Law and Images

Art and Law

Volumes published in this Brill Research Perspectives title are listed at *brill.com/rpal*

Law and Images

By

Thomas Dreier

BRILL

LEIDEN | BOSTON

This paperback book edition is simultaneously published as issue 3.1 (2019) of *Art and Law*,
DOI:10.1163/24684309-12340007

Library of Congress Control Number: 2019944025

Typeface for the Latin, Greek, and Cyrillic scripts: “Brill”. See and download: brill.com/brill-typeface.

ISBN 978-90-04-41107-4 (paperback)
ISBN 978-90-04-41109-8 (e-book)

This book is printed on acid-free paper and produced in a sustainable manner.

Printed by Printforce, the Netherlands

Contents

Law and Images

Thomas Dreier

Abstract

Law and images are generally regarded as two separate areas. Yet, in many ways law and images intersect, such as when legal rules try to control the production, dissemination and consumption of images, and when law is the subject of images. In parallel to the well-established "law and literature", the paper attempts to connect two fields of research, law studies and visual studies, that are usually disjointed, and it outlines what could be an area of interdisciplinarity research labelled "law and images". The article explains how images work to the readers not familiar with visual sciences, and how normative prohibitions and commandments function to readers not familiar with law studies. In addition, the article provides a survey of the different issues raised when studying the complex relationship between law and images.

Keywords

law – images – interdisciplinarity

1 Introduction

With the advent of television and the Internet, and especially following the spread of networked mobile devices and social networking platforms, the importance of images has dramatically increased in everyday communication and the exchange of information. Yet, from Plato's critique of pictures to an understanding of images as not just inanimate objects, but independent subjects with a life of their own, viewers have remained suspicious of images. This holds even true after the "iconic", "pictorial" or "visualistic" turn.[1] The reason for this

1 For the "iconic" turn see Boehm (2006), p. 11 et seq.; for the "pictorial" turn see Mitchell (1992); on the demarcation of the two concepts, which both try to find out how images create meaning, and how likewise to deal with images as role models for texts, see Boehm and

 | DOI:10.1163/9789004411098_002

continuing scepticism seems to be found in the dual character of depictions. As pictures, they are material objects, whereas as images they have an immaterial nature that allows them to disassociate themselves from the media – both material and immaterial – which represent them. Moreover, depictions represent something that is not present at the place and at the time when they are looked at. Most importantly, however, images are powerful, but the meaning of images is not always very clear. According to a proverb often quoted "a picture says more than a thousand words." But the question is: What exactly does it say? And how can its meaning be controlled?

This gives rise to enquire how the law reacts or should react to the proliferation of the creation and use of images made in social communication in the light of both their semantic blurriness and their possibly normative effect. In other words, because images play an important role in contemporary social communication, the legal regulation of their production, distribution and consumption is well worth being studied. This firstly brings to the centre of attention the plethora of legal rules which have as their object human actions concerning images (pornography regulation, copyright law, freedom of the arts, to name but a few). However, "regulation of images" can not only be read as a *genitivus objectivus*, but likewise as a *genitivus subjectivus*. In other words, images are not only objects of normative regulation by law, but as subjects they are likewise capable of possessing and exercising normative effects.

Discussing both these aspects transcends the narrow view of a *genitivus objectivus* and its focus on the existing legal norms regulating the production, dissemination and consumption of images which is the only issue generally dealt with in legal literature. It is postulated that focussing, in addition, on the *genitivus subjectivus* offers the possibility to establish a new research field of "law and images", which, as such, has received only little attention so far.[2] In a way, "law and images" mirrors the rather fruitful research field of "law and literature", which – rather than focusing on legal texts and their self-referential creation, dogmatic consistency and practical application – examines the qualities of legal texts and speech acts in connection with legal proceedings *as* literature as well as the representation of law *in* literature and,

---

Mitchell in: Belting (2007), pp. 27 et seq. and 37 et seq.; Sachs-Hombach (1993); on the "iconic turn" see also Maar/Burda (2004).

2 For notable exceptions, however, see especially Douzinas/Nead (1999); Joly/Visman/Weitin (2007); Dahlberg (2012); Goodrich (2013) and (2017); Manderson (2018). – Of course, more than a few papers have been published on individual issues, most notably on images of law.

to some extent also about literature as law.[3] Following, even if there are hardly any pictures to be found in legal texts, the question of "*images in law*" may nevertheless be raised, in particular if one is to expand the notion of "images" to also include non-imaging signs, such as traffic signs and the schematic representations of legal relationships.[4] Of course, "*law in images*" is a much broader area to be examined, since it ranges from images which both represent and substitute for the presence of political rules, via representations of the Last Judgement, allegorical and symbolic representations of the law as reflected in a variety of emblems, symbolic figures such as Lady Justice and more abstract symbolic signs like that of the scales, the paragraph sign (in Germany) and the hammer of the judge (in the Anglo-American legal system) up to the presentation of trial dramas in film and television.[5] In addition, one may ask to what extent images themselves can have a normative force or effect so that they might be considered as forming part of the law in a broad sense ("*images as law*"). In this respect, once again traffic signs come to mind, which as administrative acts pronounce a legal command that is to be obeyed by road users. But even generally speaking, images can be used not only to illustrate normative facts and by doing so reinforce their normative effect. Rather, it is submitted for discussion that images can themselves possess a normative effect in that their presence is intended to influence upon the behaviour of the viewer. Finally, one might ask to what extent legal rules can themselves be regarded as images or, at least, to what extent images are forming the basis of legal rules ("*law as images*"). Of course, even if the image quality of law may have been obvious at a time when images preceded writing and when law was unthinkable without images,[6] the perspective of "law as images" will probably surprise many of the traditional lawyers, since it seems to be at odds with law's traditional medium of speech and text. However, it can be demonstrated that since it is possible to regard law, and particularly legal norms, as models of reality, i.e.

3 For an earlier overview see, e.g., Posner (2009), and for new developments Hiebaum/Knaller/Pichler (2015); Anker/Meyler (2017). – For the rather reserved reception of "law and literature" in German legal literature, see Lachenmaier (2008); more openly towards interdisciplinarity, however, Baer (2011).

4 For discussion on this point, see below 2.1 and 5.1.

5 See 5.2.

6 Regarding images, symbols and writing in religion and society in the early times of the history of civilization see Haarmann (1990); to sacred objects Kohl (2003); and to the relationship between law and image see Joly, in: Joly/Vismann/Weitin (2007), p. 11.

either of the reality as it exists, or as it is envisaged by the legislature, these models which underlie legal norms might indeed be understood as images.[7]

As far as the methodologies are concerned, "law and images" explicitly transcends law's own internal perspective. Rather, beyond mere legal ways of interpretation this field of research includes methods of visual and cultural studies. It is an attempt to connect two fields of research – law studies and visual studies – that are usually disjointed. Moreover, like "law and literature", "law and images" assumes that law is not an isolated institution overarching all other social and cultural institutions, but that one would have to properly understand law as only one element embedded in the social and economic and cultural context, and hence as one of several parallel cultural phenomena.[8] Both regulating and being embedded in technologically induced and economically organized social behaviour, law will on the one hand have to react to the changes in view of digital images, networking and automated, self-learning autonomous image-generating systems. On the other hand, regarding images, the question to be asked is how legal regulation by means of text will change the way in which images are handled under those same technological and economic circumstances. For the time being, it seems that law resists images as much as images tend to elude legal regulation.

To address the issues raised in this introduction, the paper does not undertake to come up with a new original theory on either law or images. Rather, it is the purpose of this paper to "map" the territory of the area of research labelled "law and images". The reader who is not a specialist in image sciences shall be familiarized with the characteristics of images, and the non-lawyer with the operation of the law. To this effect the paper begins with a brief explanation of how images "function" as well as a brief overview of what is meant by "law" (parts 2.1 and 2.2). This includes a comparison of the different media of language and the visual (subpart 2.3). The paper then focuses on the character of normative rules, both as far as they prohibit and command certain behaviour (part 3). Since digital and networking technologies have immensely altered our understanding as well as our use of images, the changes resulting for both images and legal rules will be explored in a separate part (part 4). Following, the discussion of "law and images" would be incomplete without mapping the field of images in law, of law and for law (part 5). Concluding, the crosswise

7 For discussion see 6.2.

8 This is probably the reason why "law as culture" was chosen as the name for the Käte Hamburger center for advanced study in Bonn, Germany (http://www.recht-als-kultur.de/en/). – For additional discussion of law as only one of societies' institutions see below, 2.2.

entanglement of law and images will be explained both regarding the normative effect of images as well as the image quality of legal norms (part 6).

2 "Images", "Law"

2.1 *Images*

Like the image sciences,[9] the research field of "law and images" must first agree on the meaning of the concept of "images". This concerns the very fundamental question of image theory, i.e. the question of "what is meant by something being addressed as an image or what characteristics this object must have in order to be an image".[10] At first glance, it may seem appropriate to define an "image" as a "visual illustration of a (fictitious or real) fact, … which is material, which as a rule is visually perceptible, artificial and relatively permanent".[11]

However, already this initial definition casts certain doubts, since in focussing on the "material" character of the image, it does on the one hand not distinguish between the image, which is considered in this paper as an immaterial entity, and its material embodiment, for which, as noted in the introduction, the English language has the word "picture" ready. On the other hand, the focus on the material object which embodies an image tends to blur the line between seeing something face-to-face and seeing something in the form of an image.

Moreover, the discussion in the visual sciences[12] has shown that the forms in which images occur as visually perceptible phenomena are so diverse and different from each other that a uniform definition that sharply delimits the

9 For the constitution of image sciences, especially also in relation to traditional art history see Sachs-Hombach (2005) and (2005b); to a preliminary interim summing up see Belting (2007); on the disciplinary positioning see Rimmele/Sachs-Hombach/Stiegler (2014); on methods of visual science see Wiesing (2005a); see also the Netzwerk Bildphilosophie (2014); on methodological approaches to the exploration of visual communication see Müller (2003), pp. 121 et seq.; Sachs-Hombach/Schirra (2013); for a general overview of the different approaches within the framework of visual culture see Rimmele/Stiegler (2012); on the relationship between conceptual-philosophical and empirical-psychological approaches see Sachs-Hombach/Totzke (2011); and, finally, more cautious in order not to break off the connection to painting see Wyss (2006).

10 Wiesing (2008), p. IV (translation of the original German quotation by the author).

11 Sachs-Hombach (2005a), pp. 12–13 (translation of the original German quotation by the author).

12 On the question of the concept of the "image" in the visual sciences, see Sachs-Hombach (2013) and (2005a), pp. 12 et seq.; Wiesing (2005), pp. 9 et seq; Schulz (2005), pp. 79 et seq; Prange (2003); Müller (2003), pp. 18 et seq; Pichler/Ubl (2014); for the formulation of a comprehensive grammatology of images see Weigel (2015).

concept of the image from that of non-images has not yet been found and probably will never be found. According to Hans Belting "we not only speak in the same way about very different images", but "we also apply very different modes of discourse to the same kinds of images."[13] At the same time, the question of the concept of the image as well as the question of which images are legally regulated is, in categorical terms, "not about the exploration of what is already categorized, but about the exploration of categorization".[14] Instead of speaking of "image", it is therefore more purposeful to speak of "the images"[15] or more generally of "pictorial phenomena" as visual phenomena, whose respective descriptions can only be temporarily valid systematization attempts i.e. not definitions, but "competing proposals whose usefulness" – in relation to specific questions – "must prove".[16] This is notwithstanding the fact that the philosophy of images is in search of universally accepted truths with regard to the activity of seeing, depicting and perceiving depictions and visual information.[17] Thus, rather than asking what "is" an image the question is what should be understood as an "image" for purposes of "law and images". As explained in the introduction, the focus of "law and images" is on images as objects of normative regulation and on the normative effect that may be exercised by images, as well as on images in law and law as it appears in images.

In view of this it seems appropriate to firstly focus on images that depict a real-life object (as in the case of most of photography and to some extent also in painting) or that represent imaginary objects that could or could not exist in real life (as in many paintings). In brief and somewhat simplified without retracing here the subtle depths of the different philosophical analyses of resemblance, depiction and representation,[18] a distinction is at least to be made between the "picture" as material object, and the "image" which can be seen in the picture and which depicts or represents a real-life or imaginary object. It should be noted, however, that not all languages make this distinction between material object and the visual appearance of the object which can be seen in a picture (in the German language, e.g., the term "Bild" refers to both a

13 Belting (2001/2011), p. 9 of the English and p. 11 of the German edition, with further references.

14 Wiesing (2005), p. 14 (translation of the original German quotation by the author).

15 Schulz (2005), p. 30.

16 Sachs-Hombach (2005a), p. 13 (translation of the original German quotation by the author).

17 For an overview from the German perspective, see especially Boehm (2007).

18 For an extensive overview of resemblance as well as conventional and psychological theories of "depiction" see Hyman/Bantinaki (2017) with references to the English language philosophical literature, especially Wollheim (1980), Hopkins (1998) and Walton (1990) (not listing, however, important foreign language sources).

"picture" and an "image"). Following – and again without going into detail – a distinction is to be made between (a) an object depicted, (b) a depiction of that object in a physical form, and (c), the immaterial image that can be seen in a picture of an object depicted.

In addition, since production and viewing of images are at the same time embedded in a communicative context the legislator intends to regulate, the viewer's gaze must also be considered, both in terms of the "pre"- and "after"-images inscribed in the memory of both the image creator and the viewer, and whose existence is overwritten, supplemented, expanded and modified by each further consumption of a new image.[19] What is meant in this context by "after-image" is not the image that physiologically continues to appear in one's vision after the exposure to the original image has ceased. Rather reference is made here to the image in the form in which it is remembered by the person who saw it. Correspondingly, such an after-image inscribed in the viewer's visual memory becomes a "pre-image" if it is remembered and used as the basis for the creation of a new image. Although these purely mental images are not always taken into consideration in the image sciences,[20] their inclusion seems nevertheless meaningful from the point of view of visual sciences and particularly from the legal point of view, because without taking them into account it is not possible to explain the detachment of immaterial images from their production or their medial circulation once the images are liberated from their original content having become transporters of visual concepts outside of themselves.[21] In this way, the cycle of wandering images as produced and seen by individual viewers and stored in a society's collective memory is finally closed, where iconic images contribute to and form part of collective narratives which in turn contribute to shaping a group identity in the same way as they become role models for actions as well as the production and understanding of new images.[22] Stored and handed down in collective memory, the

19 On the mental character of images which are received by the medium of the human visual apparatus as an external image and subsequently generated as an internal image, see Belting (2001/2011), pp. 15 et seq. and 37 et seq. of the English and pp. 19 et seq. and pp. 57 et seq. of the German edition; the neurological aspects are explained, e.g., by Kandel (2012); Vogeley (2005); Hoffmann (1998); on the different approaches to what constitutes perception see, e.g., Wiesing (2002), and on experiential as well as on recognition-based theories of depiction Hyman/Bantinaki (2017).

20 Sachs-Hombach, in: Sachs-Hombach (2005), p. 13. – For an inclusion of mental images, however, Belting (2001/2011), pp. 15 et seq. of the English and pp. 19 et seq. of the German edition; Weigel (2015), pp. 9 et seq.; already earlier Sontag (1977); Flusser (1984).

21 Bruhn (2007).

22 On icons in the collective memory of German people see Thiele (2005); on indexing and interpreting the world through pictures see Blasche/Gutmann/Weingarten (2004);

best-known iconic images are even so strongly internalized that they can be remembered from visual memory solely by means of a textual description.[23]

Secondly, without doubt, the focus of "law and images" is first and foremost on depictions which are produced by way of photographs.[24] This is simply due to the actual frequency with which photos are taken each day millions of times mostly by digital cameras in smartphones. However, merely focusing on photographs would disregard other artefacts which depict real-life objects and were hence considered as "mirrors of the world",[25] or which represent objects that could be real or may just be imagined. Such artefacts were also subject to legal regulation in many ways. Normative requirements existed both regarding craftsmanship and the choice of subject matter and image composition. It suffices, here, to just mention the instructions for the correct production of colours and paintings in the early 12th century work "De diversis artibus" by the Benedictine monk Theophilus Presbyter. Likewise, normative power can be ascribed to the well accepted rule according to which donor figures were to be depicted smaller in size than the saints depicted. Similarly, within the framework of Christian iconography the attributes of the saints necessary for their identification were also defined by conventions. Moreover, the depiction of the content was also subject to normative expectations, as can be seen in the replacement of the initial title of Veronese's "Last Supper" painted in 1573, which the Inquisition considered to be too worldly a depiction, by the more harmless pictorial designation "The Feast in the House of Levi".

But from a "law and images" perspective, the notion of the "image" should be even wider.

To begin with, in view of the long tradition of symbolic and emblematic representations of law and legal facts, the visual symbols and emblems which "allow the inherent logic of the images to be recognised and to act for the law" should likewise be included, since, firstly, symbols often represent objects such

---

Harth/Steinbrenner (2013); Herder (2017); on the efficiency of photography in this context see the positions at Boström/Jäger (2004).

23 Examples of such images are listed in Presse Informations AG (2004), pp. 9 et seq. (e.g., "Footprint of the first man on the moon", "Ché Guevarra smoking a cigar", and many more).

24 For a comprehensive description of photography, its functions and uses see Stiegler (2006a); Rouillé (2005); Geimer (2009); for positions of photographic theory see the source collections of writings on photography by Kemp (1980–1983) and v. Amelunxen (2000), as well as of Stiegler (2010); on photographic metaphors see Stiegler (2006); on the relationship between photography and painting Wyss (2006); Pohlmann/v. Hohenzollern (2004); Beiersdorf (2018).

25 On realistic Dutch landscapes and genre painting close to images see Belting (1994); on the psychology of visual representation see Gombrich (1959) and (1982).

as "law" by depicting things that do have shapes and colours, and, secondly, it is possible to infer from symbols "approaches to a legal theory of images" which ultimately permit "a productive coexistence of image and text".[26]

Moreover, visual representations that appear to be illustrations but that represent objects or phenomena which are not visible to the human eye should likewise be considered. This category includes above all scientific images,[27] in which the objects depicted are only visible to the human eye after they have been magnified, or in which data not perceptible to the human eye are made visible, such as in the case of the visualization of data collected by satellites on the weather or the background noise of the universe. These data are translated into visual information according to certain conventions, which, if followed, make the visual representation of the data look like a traditional photograph, but the aim of which is to evoke associations in the observer by means of which he or she grasps the meaning of what is depicted. In other words, in these cases it is not important what the viewer sees, but what he thinks he is seeing. In such a broad sense, the term image then refers to "a[ny] spatial distribution of a physical property such as radiation, electric charge, conductivity, or reflectivity, mapped from another distribution of either the same or another physical property".[28]

However, even this broad definition still emphasises the activity of "transfer" or "mapping". In doing so, it neither addresses the material object embodying the image, nor does it encompass images such as construction drawings, computer-generated images and implementations of data which do not represent physical objects. In view of the possibility to digitally create unreal objects and worlds which only appear to be realistic depictions, dealing with images should also include artificial images that have no actual correlation to the real world, but only a potential one. From the perspective of "law and images" it is then interesting to study to what extent a legal norm applies to the representation (or simply presentation) of a certain object in a picture, or whether the norm addresses the special way in which this representation (or presentation) is made.

Also, another extension of the term "image" as referred to in "law and images" seems to be called for. In order not to exclude image commandments from being considered, which are included in the law by way of signs, "law

26 Vismann (2007), pp. 27–28 (translation of the original German quotation by the author); extensively Goodrich (2013) and (2017).

27 Vögtli/Ernst (2007); Liebsch/Mößner (2012); on purely technical imaging techniques see Mittelberger/Pelz/Rosen/Franke (2013).

28 Mensa (1992).

and images" should also consider signs – including pictograms oscillating between symbolic signs and depicting images – which in addition to their signal character also embody a normative appeal. This is irrespective of the fact that it may be subject to discussion whether each sign is likewise an image and whether each image is, at the same time, a sign, or whether images are to be characterized as signs close to perception.[29] From the formal point of view of semiotics, which is based on the trichotomic relationship between thing, concept and symbol, it is in any case irrelevant whether the symbol assumes the form of text, of a sign or of a pictorial representation (in the language of semiotics, an "icon") of a real or fictitious object. However, since the relationship between a sign and what it stands for is always arbitrary and determined by an agreement, the normative character of the definition contained in this agreement can also be considered when undertaking studies on "law and images".

Finally, it might seem appropriate to also consider models of reality. Even if quite like signs, models may not usually be regarded as images in the narrow sense, they do, however, share with depictions the characteristics of mapping and transferring from reality to the model. Indeed, to include models in research concerned with "law and images" makes sense insofar as models are underlying automated applications which – such as face recognition techniques – are used to automatically process data for the enforcement of legal norms.[30] Also, as demonstrated towards the end of this paper,[31] the model of reality underlying a legal norm brings legal norms close to what might be considered, in a very broad sense, as an image.

In sum, for the purposes of the research field "law and images", no conclusive definition of what "is" an image is required. In contrast to image theory, the question of what constitutes an object so that it can be spoken of as an image is not at the centre of interest of this field of research. Rather, from the cognitive interest of "law and images", the concept of the image should be so broadly defined that it encompasses all visually perceptible artefacts which can be said to be either depictions, symbols and emblems, signs or models

29 See Schulz (2005), pp. 102 et seq.; Boehme-Neßler (2010), pp. 58–59. – Also, authors of philosophy have at times been stated that the question of whether images are signs is in any case not a question of characteristics, but rather one of their functional use; see Wiesing (2005), pp. 37 et seq.; on the sign-theoretical foundations see Nöth (2005); Blanke/Giannone/Vaillant (2005); however, there are many other authors who have a different view on this issue; see, especially the discussion of broadly understood "symbols" by Goodman (1968/1976).

30 See below, 5.3.

31 See below, 6.2.

that can be the subject of legal regulation; from which, as subject, a normative commandment or at least a normative appeal can emanate; which concern an issue of normativity; or which influence upon the creation and design of legal norms.

Of course, finally one may well ask whether the distinction just proposed can be said to be a generally valid anthropological description, independent of time and place, or whether this view of the images is not itself culturally influenced. To answer this question, it should probably be recalled that what objects are today considered as images, is the result of a centuries-long debate[32] which in Europe, but not in other places, was largely based on canon law. Hence, one may well doubt the universal validity of the understanding of "images" presented here. On a side line, it might be added that it has been suggested that seeing does not only follow optical and neuroscientific laws, but at least in part depends on language and is thus culturally influenced.[33] However, as Hans Belting has explained, it seems possible to assume an anthropologically determined use and understanding of images, if one understands "anthropological" not in the way of a temporally immovable constant, but in the sense that across time, space and culture every image perception is as such "an act of animation" and a "symbolic action", even if it may be "practiced in very different ways in different cultures or in today's image techniques". In other words, what remains constant is the fact that people deal with images, since "we are not the master of our images, but rather ... at their mercy".[34] In contrast, what is changeable is the practice of images, i.e. the generation of images and the handling of images in social space as well as in relation to time, space and different cultures. This is the reason why "the question of what an image is remains a rather narrow inquiry so long as it does not explore the notion of images in cultures other than our own", that is as long discussion is limited to the "invisible horizon of Western thought and Western experience".[35]

---

32 For the iconoclastic controversy, see, e.g., Belting (1997), pp. 146 et seq.; Freedberg (1989), pp. 378 et seq.; on the Christian prohibition of images up to the cult of relics see Kohl (2003), pp. 31 et seq.

33 Whether seeing depends on concepts and language or is instead informationally encapsulated is an open question which is usually discussed under the label "conceptual penetration of perception"; see Robbins (2017). For an example of the influence of language on the perception of colour see Deutscher (2010).

34 Belting (2001/2011), p. 9 of the English and p. 12 of the German edition ("erscheint der Mensch nicht als Herr seine Bilder, sondern ... als 'Ort der Bilder', die seinen Körper besetzen").

35 Belting (2001/2011), p. 32 of the English, and p. 50 of the German edition.

2.2 *Law*

Looking at the other of the two concepts of "law and images", it has to be ascertained what exactly is addressed as a social phenomenon when one speaks about "the law". Of course, although literature in the field of legal theory, philosophy and methodology is abundant, for the purposes of this article, which just undertakes to lay the groundwork for "law and images" as a field of research, a few general explanations must suffice.

2.2.1 Law: a Working Definition

When speaking about "law and images", the term "law" refers first and foremost to the body of statutory norms enacted in a legal procedure by a legislature empowered to do so.[36] Such norms enacted by the legislative body competent to do so are characterized by the fact that in the event of non-compliance the command contained in the legal statutory rule can be enforced against the will of the norm addressee with the aid of state enforcement assistance. It is of importance, in this respect, that particularly in the Western states characterised by enlightenment and secularisation, the law has not only detached itself from its sacral and religious roots in a long historical development, but at the same time the enforcement of basic concepts of order by means of criminal law has separated itself from the regulation of private and commercial issues by means of civil law.[37] Whereas norms of criminal law aim at the protection of supra-individual collective legal interests, civil law norms endeavour to resolve conflict situations between private legal subjects. From this distinction, it follows that the sovereign initiative to prosecute violations of the law lies with the public prosecutor's office in the case of criminal offenses and with the civil parties in the case of private tort claims as well as in the case of broken contractual promises. Of course, this fundamental distinction between criminal law on the one hand and civil law on the other does not rule out the possibility that mixed forms have survived, such as where an application by the injured private party is required to actuate the state prosecution of the violation of a criminal law prohibition. A similar link exists in jurisdictions in which the

36 For a list of the different areas of law in which legal rules concerning images are to be found see 3.1 and 3.2.

37 For the remaining entanglements, see, e.g., in German civil law § 823 para. 2 of the German Civil Code (Bürgerliches Gesetzbuch, BGB), according to which civil law liability for damages is also ordered if a criminal law provision which is intended to also protect interests of individuals was infringed; see also § 106 of the German Copyright Act (Urheberrechtsgesetz, UrhG), according to which every civil copyright infringement is in principle at the same time also a criminal offense.

prosecutor's office's is empowered to refer the infringed person to pursue a criminal lawsuit in that person's private capacity.

Moreover, in countries which allow for a constitutional control of ordinary laws enacted by Parliament, both ordinary civil and criminal laws must be interpreted in the light of fundamental rights as enshrined, in Europe, in both the European Convention on Human Rights and the Charter of Fundamental Rights as well as in national Constitutions. Regarding "law and images" this means that statutory rules and ordinances or administrative decisions on images by the state administration are to be measured against fundamental rights, especially against the freedom of expression and the freedom of the press, and against the freedom of the arts. However, fundamental rights which favour the making, dissemination and consumption of visual material are not the only fundamental rights protected. Rather, conflicting fundamental rights such as especially the protection of privacy, which protects the persons depicted, and the protection of physical and immaterial property, which protects those who produce and deal in images, are to be considered. In legal practice, this leads to a balancing of these conflicting fundamental rights undertaken by the courts on a case by case basis. Of course, in view of the mostly general wording of the individual fundamental rights and because of the incommensurability of the conflicting fundamental rights such a balancing is not an easy task.[38]

Most important, it has to be noted that all legal rules are only "ought" norms, i.e. they only describe how the addressees of the respective norms should behave, but they do not already carry their observance within themselves.[39] What is needed in order to comply with the normative command of a statutory norm is either a voluntary decision of the norm addressee to act in accordance with the legislative command, or state coercion which enforces the correct behaviour or restores the desired state of things, such as when, e.g., images that are in violation of a general or a specific ban on images (pornography legislation; infringements of copyright) are being destroyed. It should be noted, however, that the character of a legal rule as an "ought" norm vanishes whenever digital access controls and technical protection measures are used. In these cases, the rule enforced is no longer about what *should* be done, but it already defines from the outset by way of the restraints embedded in the algorithm which acts *can* de facto be performed. In other words, whenever the limits of the freedom to act is defined by digital technology, the norm addressees

38 For discussion, see, e.g., in German legal literature the commentaries to Art. 5 Abs. 3 GG; Würkner (1994); Korinek (2006); Ladeur (2007).

39 See only Hoerster (2006), pp. 36 et seq.

cannot behave any differently than it is prescribed by the norm that has been implemented by technical means. At present, such technical devices are not so much used by democratic states, but rather to an increasing extent by private parties who define the conditions according to which their digitised products and services can be used. Thus, image producers, image agencies and image platform operators may determine, by way of technical access and use controls, the way in which the images offered can be viewed, duplicated, distributed and otherwise disseminated. How the legislature can react to this new phenomenon made possible by digital technology will be further discussed below.[40]

Moreover, from the view point of "law and images" the term "law" should not be limited to state law. Rather, social norms should likewise be encompassed, even if from a legal perspective, social norms are not regarded as being part of the law due to the lack of the possibility of their enforcement by state coercion. But like truly legal norms, social norms also have a normative content, because social norms also contain a demand or at least an appeal that the norm addressee shall behave as intended, even if only non-legal, social sanctions are available in cases of non-compliance with a social norm. To illustrate this difference between state legal norms and social norms by an example: The person who has been commissioned to take a photograph and who subsequently delivers a blurry image is obliged to pay damages according to the provisions of the warranty as specified in statutory law and in the contract. Should the photographer then refuse to pay the sums of money required, the commissioning party can recover them after having obtained a judgement which can subsequently be enforced with the help of the coercive means of the state. In contrast, a person who is asked by his acquaintance to take a photograph owes nothing in the legal sense. If the photograph is blurred, at the next occasion the person asking will only look for another photographer.

When it comes to "law and images", the notion of "law" can even be understood in yet a wider sense including even normative appeals that are inherent in images once the images are shown to the onlooker or to the casual passer-by. Quite like in the case of state legal norms and social norms, the expectation associated with the showing of the picture is aimed at initiating a certain reaction in the viewer. Only such a wide understanding of "the law" may cover normative claims that are transported via images, such as is the case mainly in advertising, but also whenever, and to the degree in which, images serve the purpose of, or are being used for, the constructions of images of the self.

Such a broad understanding of "the law" as comprising normative rules, social norms and pictorial appeals to the viewer of images that make a normative

40 See part 4.2.

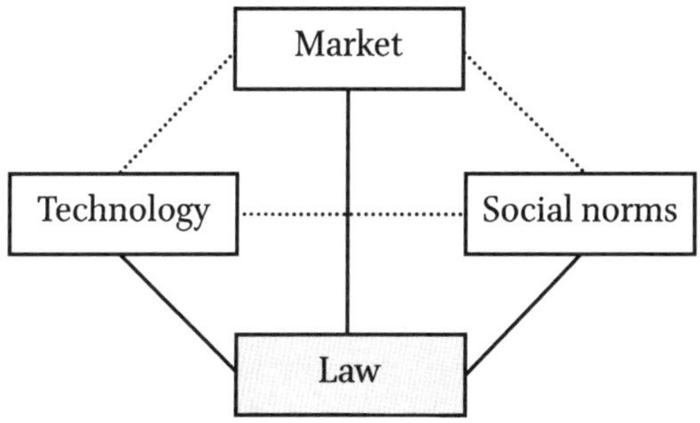

FIGURE 1 Law in the context of other social subsystems (solid lines: interaction with participation of law; dotted lines: interaction without participation of law)

claim seems well justified if one takes into consideration that law is, after all, only one of several social subsystems. Contrary to the understanding particularly in countries whose legal system is rooted in Roman law and who tend to think that the legal solution to every present and future individual case is predetermined by the legal norms themselves,[41] the influence of law within society is by no means as comprehensive as generally assumed by lawyers. This is well demonstrated by the diagram shown in Fig. 1 which takes Luhmann's description of the main functional systems of society[42] as a starting point – disregarding, however, as Lessig did for purposes of greater clarity, the subsystems religion and science as well as the autopoietic isolation of the individual systems – and which schematically illustrates that law is by no means involved in all interrelationships between the individual social subsystems of law, social norms, technology and the market.

What is illustrated in Fig. 1 may be demonstrated by just one recent example. It is only some years ago that technical engineers connected the wireless telephone to the Internet and equipped it with a camera. This combination, the demand for which the technicians could only guess at first, has developed into what is known today as the smartphone which had an unprecedented success on the market. At the same time, it was leading to new types of images such as "selfies", "party photos" and the like. All these developments were as such not regulated, i.e., neither promoted nor hindered by the law. Likewise, legal norms had no influence on the consequences of the playful use the users

41 See, e.g., Engisch (2010), p. 45 ("continuously be subject to the law with our actions"; translation of the original German quotation by the author).

42 Luhmann (1997/2003) and (1993/2004); Lessig (1999), pp. 87 et. seq.

were making of this new technical device, although these new uses lastingly changed the social conventions of interpersonal visual communication as well as communication in general. Legal action was only initiated, once – and to the extent – the technology-induced changes in behaviour began to get out of hand and violations of traditional values such as that of privacy (e.g., voyeuristic recordings) and human dignity (e.g., cyberbullying) could be observed.

Finally, it should be noted that the full impact of normative rules at the crossroads of "law and images" can only be grasped if one does not limit the normative rules to be considered to positively formulated norms. Rather, in order to gain a proper understanding of the regulation of images and the visual, opposing normative claims to validity have also to be taken into account, such as those motivating graffiti sprayers and street artists who, by deliberately disregarding and challenging the rules of the law governing images, resist the prevailing aesthetics supported by legal rules, according to which graffiti tags and street art sprays are nothing more than a visual disfigurement of the public sphere. If one were to leave out these counter-claims to the prevailing aesthetics and the legal rules supporting them, the important issue of power and sovereignty over the visual design of the public space and the clash of ownership interests and the interest of freedom of action could not be addressed.[43]

2.2.2 Law and Ethics

Beyond the mere contents of existing legal regulation, its inner functioning and mechanism of its application, an additional important issue of "law and images" is the issue of the relationship between legal norms regulating the production, use and consumption of images on the one hand, and ethical rules on the other hand.

This issue has two aspects, the first of which is the general question to what extent the content of legal rules that have been adopted in accordance with the formal procedure provided for their adoption can be said to be in conformity with ethical rules, i.e. to what extent and under which circumstances a specific legal rule is to be judged as either ethical or unethical. This general debate cannot be retracted here in detail. Rather, it shall only briefly be mentioned that the answer to this question touches upon the question whether a legal norm should reflect and help stabilize moral attitudes or whether it should be applied with the aim of correcting them. In addition, it can be concluded with some certainty that not many legal norms which have to be described as unethical will be found in States which provide for a strong protection of

43 Banksy (2006).

fundamental human rights, since the formulation as well as the interpretation of human rights is in general to a large extent based on ethical arguments.[44]

The second aspect is whether a particular "image ethics" can be formulated, i.e. whether it is possible to formulate principles according to which it can be determined which actions of producing, disseminating, making visible, placing in context and looking at images morally right or morally wrong.[45] To the extent such an image ethics can be formulated, the existing legal image rules can be examined as to whether – and if so, to what extent – they comply with these ethical rules. From the point of view of a consequentialist ethics, such rules can probably be constructed assuming that it can have negative consequences if certain persons such as especially children and adolescents are faced with images of a certain sexual nature or violence. The construction of images of women in advertising, as well as images that lead to dangerous or socially harmful behaviour could also be grounds for the formulation of ethical rules for images.[46] However, as the case of so-called ego-shooter games has demonstrated, care must be taken not to prematurely assume causal relationships that merely support the image preferences of those who seek to enforce a particular rule for images.[47] In deontological terms, however, it seems more difficult to formulate a universally valid image ethics. After all, at times the historically evolved rules of images in the individual cultures differ considerably from one another, think only of the cultural differences relating to the depiction and public visualization of the (unclothed) human body. This is a strong indication that image rules are contingent rather than constant over time and space. Only a small number of rules regulating images are to be found that can claim to have universal validity, such as the ban on child pornography.[48]

2.3 *Language and Text versus Visual Representation*

Obviously, the relationship between law and image paradigmatically represents the rivalry between textual and visual information. Following early forms of normative representation of imperial power and the imperial office by way

44 For a more detailed discussion of this last point, see, e.g., Dreier (2018).

45 For an example see the collection of essays edited by Gross/Katz/Ruby (2003).

46 For the construction of the image of women in the wider societal context see only Wolf (1990).

47 See, e.g., Sörensen (2018); for an empirical study on the effects of web pages with sexual content on adolescents see Grimm/Rhein/Müller (2010).

48 Optional Protocol to the Convention on the Rights of the Child on the Sale of Children, Child Prostitution and Child Pornography (UN Treaty Series, vol. 2171, p. 227 (247)), in force since 18 February 2002 and signed by 121 states. – On the changing understanding of what used to be referred to as "morality offences" up to the beginning of the 20th century see Quanter (1925/2003); on the interface between body and art Zimmermann (2001).

of images which acted as veritable deputies, and after the disappearance of pictorial explanations of legal texts to those subject to the law who were unacquainted with reading,[49] writing has clearly established itself as the medium in which normative legal sentences are formulated and transported over space and time.

2.3.1 Opposition

It is true that the written nature of law, which is at the same time a written nature of memory, has a long-standing tradition in transporting normative commands not only in space, but also in time. Even if the Roman art of memory, "made the connection between memory and image strong", as Aleida Assmann put it, before all it was Roman law which by producing the Corpus Iuris Civilis emphasized the collection of laws in written form. Moreover, in the Renaissance, preference was given to writing when a choice had to be made between writing and image as memory devices. Whereas images were exposed, in the form of material pictures, to the danger of destruction, writing was understood as immaterial, even if the books which contained the written ideas were likewise vulnerable to destruction. In view of this, the two media also had a different relationship to time. Only writing was regarded as lasting over time, if it was not even regarded as standing completely outside of time. Since writing has both readability and transparency on its side, for Francis Bacon the plea for writing corresponded "with a refutation of images, which he also fought against in order to strengthen an archaic anthropomorphic mentality".[50] Even those later authors who, like Jakob Burkhardt and Aby Warburg, pleaded for the image to be upgraded as a carrier of information by claiming "the predicate of immediacy, which had been reserved for written over visual information, for images" had to concede that, unlike writing, pictures are not connected with transparency but with non-transparency and "irreducible ambivalence".[51]

Against the background of this historical development, one may well ask whether – and if so for how long – the law will be able to resist, after the "iconic" and the "pictorial turn", the massive appearance of images and maintain its hermetic shield against the images. In the future, will images outpace text in normative statements? Some authors predict that law will inevitably have to open to images, and others foresee even an erosion of text-bound law

49 For detail, see below, 5.2.

50 Assmann (1999/2003), pp. 218 et seq. (translation of the original German quotation by the author); on the competition of writing and image as memory media by Bacon and Milton, ibid., pp. 190 et seq.

51 Ibid., p. 220.

by images.[52] However, this rather seems to be a rhetorical attention-grabbing exacerbation. After all, the increasing complexity of the world cannot in the slightest be depicted by images in view of the blurred meaning of images. As a subsystem of society, law to a rather large extent has the "technical" task of generating solutions to individual, economic and social conflicts in times of an increasing differentiated demand for appropriate solutions to an increasing differentiation of individual cases and conflicts of interest. In other words, the complexity of these conflict situations correlates with the need for precise and increasingly differentiated solutions. Such differentiated solutions can, however, only be provided for by text. In view of this, the postulate that the fulfilment of this social task can be achieved by means of images appears, after all, to be nothing more than a far-fetched speculation.

But there are also reasons beyond readability and transparency, which speak in favour of writing and text as the means of choice when it comes to the law. For example, because of its clarity text is generally associated with reason, whereas images, because of the blurriness of what they show, are considered as belonging to the realm of feeling. This likewise reinforces the isolation of the law vis-à-vis the images, since law and legal decision making shall deliberately be kept free from diffuse feelings for reasons of justice as well as of comprehensibility. Without question, the isolation of the law from images is at the same time a means of safeguarding its own supremacy as a sub-system of society. The hostility of the law towards images and the self-imputed supremacy of the law when it comes to govern images are two sides of the same coin. An opening of the law to images would therefore inevitably lead to a weakening of law's supremacy over the visual. The supremacy thus lost would then have to be established in a way other than with reference to the primacy of the written nature committed to clarity and reason.

However, all these reasons pointing to and explaining the text-based nature of the law do not influence upon the extent to which the conception of legal text is preceded by mental images, and to what extent the normative language makes itself use of linguistic images. Moreover, the text-based nature of the law cannot prevent that in times of growing visual communication, there is an ever growing need to communicate the increasing internal complexity of legal judgements by way of visual representations that can easily be understood. This leads to a much greater use of pictorial material in legal communication than ever before.[53] Both these aspects can only be briefly mentioned here.

52 Boehme-Neßler (2009), pp. 144 et seq.; Goodrich (2017).

53 For visual communication by the courts see 5.2. – See also on the scope for legally permitted litigation PR Boehme-Neßler (2010).

2.3.2 Entanglements

But the relationship between text and image in law cannot be described as one of opposition alone. Quite to the contrary, it is likewise possible to focus on the manifold interrelationships between textual and visual communication within normative rules.[54]

Firstly, in all religiously and ideologically motivated societies, which tightly control which images may not be seen and which images shall be looked at, this differentiation is maintained not only by way of physically withholding pictures and demonstratively showing others in places where they cannot be overlooked, but it is generally enforced with the help of the law. Hence, both images and the laws that control them form an integral part of the visual policy pursued.

In a general way, however, in addition to the immaterial ideas they transport, both handwriting and the printed typeface are, of course, not images in themselves. However, concrete poetry has aimed at giving the visual arrangement of the text the form of an image, thus not only adding another layer of semantic meaning but also interweaving text and image. Also, in cases in which normative acts are automatically performed, such as in the case of an automated contract, this results in a transformation of the written contract language first into a model of the relationships of the parties involved, their transactions and legal consequences, which underlies the algorithm, and which is, in a second step, transformed back into text written in the respective programming language. If one understands, as explained above,[55] a model as an image in the wider sense, automated contracts can indeed be considered another example of an entanglement of text and image.

Moreover, it is only possible to discuss images by means of language, but not by means of other images, even if in art history since Aby Warburg's Bilderatlas "Mnemosyne" several attempts have been made to put forward an argument even without words just simply by the juxtaposition and arrangement of images alone.[56] True, the awareness of the specific argumentative potential of the combination of images may have been increasing. However, even the visual sciences as a rule still describe the images with texts. Moreover, in the critical humanities, the images are even literally "read" as texts, as if one were once again trying to banish the multiplicity of meanings inherent in the images

54 On the interlacing of speech and image acts, see, e.g., Seja (2009).

55 See 2.1. – For discussion of legal norms as models and hence as images in a wider sense see also 4.2.

56 On Warburg see Warnke (2003); Heil/Brehm/Ohrt (2016); on the relationship of Warburg's restitution of the image to the legal concept of subjective right see Steinhauer (2013), pp. 96 et seq.; on the recent trend of a rational argumentation by way of images see Thürlemann (2013); and on the opposition of reading and seeing see Beyer (2017).

and the subversive power subordinated to them with the help of an additional amount of text.

Even in law itself, images are often being subsumed under legal regimes that were primarily conceived for texts. A vivid example is the provision of the German Penal Code, according to which "sound and image carriers, data memories, illustrations and other representations" are subjected to the same rules as writings ("*Schriftwerke*").[57] Similarly, in the US Constitution the protection of communication via images is based solely on the freedom of speech guaranteed in the Constitution's first Amendment. However, in contrast both the European guarantees of fundamental rights and the German Basic Law ("*Grundgesetz*"), are based on the broader concept of freedom of expression which expressly addresses both writings and images.[58] In addition, in the context of freedom of expression, the image and the text surrounding the image are understood as a uniform expression of opinion in which the text attached to an image "speaks for" the image and, in case of doubt, determines the content and true meaning of the image.

A further entanglement can be found in the law of evidence. It took a comparatively long time before the photographic image of the scene of a crime was accepted as equal to and, subsequently, even as superior to the literal narrative of the eye witness in terms of accuracy to the narrated remembrance. After all, photographic evidence is only secondary evidence and thus close to hearsay which in common law jurisdictions is excluded as evidence, so that it was only permissible to use photographs to illustrate the direct testimony that was orally given. However, the answer to the question whether photographs were admissible in accordance with the rules of procedural law was never straightforward, because it was never easy to decide whether the photography presented merely illustrated the language of the witness or whether, quite to the contrary, the language of the witness explained the picture that was presented as testimony in court. Once accepted, the resulting shift of trust from oral testimony remembered at the time of trial to visual testimony recorded earlier requires an unbroken trust in the existence of a continuous indexicality between the reality depicted on the one hand, and the depiction of that reality in the resulting photograph on the other hand, which is as such not entirely unproblematic.[59]

57 § 11 Abs. 3 StGB.

58 Art. 5 (1) sentence 1 Grundgesetz (GG); Art. 11 (1) of the EU Charter of fundamental rights; Art. 10 of the European Convention on Human Rights (ECHR).

59 For German law see Karallus (2007) and Leitner (2007); for US-law Golan (2002), pp. 182 et seq.

While both images and law were initially closely connected, so that law could not be thought of and staged without images, a "desynchronization of image and law" took place from the Middle Ages to the present day. It was this desynchronization that has resulted in the present understanding of the law as a purely written medium hostile to images. At the same time, it fell into oblivion that legal and visual rhetorical codes overlap, that there are not only rules of law "that standardize an image", but also "rules of the image that govern the law". Thus, the discussion of law and images, of images and law is about the "image regime of law" as well as about the "legal regime of the image", i.e. about "images of law, from its own sphere, and images framed by legal rules".[60] Even though the number of legal norms that intend to regulate images can hardly be numbered, it may not be exaggerating to speak of an epoch in which the image as subject "dictates its own law to law",[61] at a time in which images have gained an importance in contemporary media communication as never before. In legal terms, both regimes mentioned, law and images, are intersected in the law of one's own image as well as in the inclusion of photographs in copyright law. This is so, because the legal protection of one's own image[62] – which has as its predecessor the royal portrait just as much as it represents the 15 minutes of fame in the media predicted by Andy Warhol to everyone – presupposes the constitution of this image just as much as the notion of photography as an art form precedes its legal qualification as an object of protection covered by copyright. Once more, the text of the statutory norm and the image it regulates appear as inextricably linked to each other.

3 Normative Regulation of Images

Legal norms which aim at containing the negative effects imputed to images have since times immemorial played a major role, most likely going as far back as to religiously motivated taboos. Although it might without doubt be worthwhile to retrace this history, before doing so the question has to be answered what types of regulations the law does provide for the regulation of visual communication.

Apart from regulatory matters such as copyright law which aim at structuring the allocation of ownership of images and the trading in images, there are essentially only two opposing types of standard commands available to the

60 Vismann (2007), pp. 15–16 ("Bildregime des Rechts" as well as "Rechtsregime des Bildes"; translation of the original German quotation by the author).

61 Joly, in: Joly/Vismann/Weitin (2007), pp. 12, 14.

62 Vismann (2007), p. 16; Steinhauer (2007), (2009) and (2013).

law. Whereas the first type of these commands, the image prohibition, comes in the form of "do not look", the second type, the image commandment, quite to the opposite confronts the viewers with the command "do look". Of course, each of these two types of standard commands is then differentiated and partly relativized, such as when only certain groups of potential viewers are normatively told either to look at a picture or not to look at it, or when a picture may only be shown under certain conditions and in certain contexts but not in others. As far as their practical application is concerned, it is to be noted that the number of image prohibitions is by far greater than the number of commandments directed at the production, dissemination and use of images.

Although at first glance image prohibitions not to look at pictures and image commandments to look at them seem to be antagonistic commands, they are nevertheless intrinsically linked to each other, since they both share the common belief in the power of images. The difference consists merely in the valuation of this power. Whereas prohibitions of images turn against the power that is imputed to images and considered harmful to the viewer, commandments to look at pictures seek, quite to the opposite, to make use of the power of images in cases in which it is considered as salutary. Moreover, the pronouncement of both prohibitions and commandments can be part of a common image policy. This can be illustrated by the Middle Ages, which the average person did not see more than a small number of pictures, and in rural areas were mostly limited to the few paintings hanging in the village church. Although it might seem that the need for normative regulation of images was comparatively small, quite the opposite was true. Just because the number of images to be seen was small, each single "false" image stuck out much more and could potentially cause – so it was believed – much greater harm than a single false image amongst the myriads of images filling cyberspace today. For this reason, the church authorities paid meticulous attention to the correct execution of pictures that should and those that should not be seen. Thus, prohibitions of certain images and commands to look at other images indeed appear to be as two sides of the same coin.

3.1 *Prohibitions*

Prohibitions which aim at regulating the production and in particular the distribution and consumption of images are numerous and they have quite different motivations.[63] According to a topos that can be traced back to antiquity, even looking at a picture is dangerous since pictures are generally

63 For a theory of image prohibitions see the contributions in Frankenberg/Niesen (2004); on a compilation of photographs, which have led, if not always to legal, but certainly to social disputes, Girardin/Pirker (2003).

not what they represent, and by pretending to be what they are not as well as by presenting as present what in reality is not present, they lie. Even if pictures do not lie and the viewer should not let himself be deceived by them, they are always only an image, a copy of reality and thus even a step further away from the truth than the object depicted which, according to Plato's idealistic understanding, is only representing the true object and therefore as such not the real thing.[64]

Just as long, if not longer, is the tradition of visual taboos. Initially religiously or ritually motivated, visual taboos still play a role today whenever it is agreed in society that certain images shall not be seen, or whenever the person in control over the visual images attempts to preserve his sole knowledge of, and thus his power over these images and the objects depicted. Interpreted in a more modern way, the taboo underlying a ban on a given type of images is motivated by the intention to prevent the viewer from a sight that would otherwise burn itself into his memory where, if once seen, it could no longer be erased. This line of tradition shows an unmistakable parallel to the prohibition of eating the fruit of the forbidden tree. Only superficially the biblical story is about eating, about a physical in contrast to an immaterial incorporation of what has been seen. For both eating and seeing are about the appropriation of some spiritual knowledge which the person who pronounced the prohibition intends to keep for himself, if only to beware the others to whom the prohibition is addressed from destructive consequences.[65] However, quite like with the apple and its appeal to be eaten, the temptation to look is always present, even if only as an anthropologically conditioned attention reflex that is so strong that it can hardly be suppressed by a conscious effort of the will. The penalties threatened and applied if the ban is violated are of a drastic nature. In the Greek saga, Orpheus, who was unable to resist the temptation to turn around before he had regained the upper world, forever lost his beloved Eurydice. In the Bible, Adam and Eve were expelled from Paradise. Today, the main examples of this type of image bans to be seen in this tradition are the normative withholding of pornographic and violent images from the eyes of children and adolescents, as well as the prohibition of the use of symbols of anti-constitutional organizations, the violation of which is likewise severely punished by way of criminal law. Of course, as mentioned above, prohibitions – and, it might be added commandments – which are based on visual taboos, may not be limited to depictions but might likewise apply to mere vision of the object depicted. For instance, the ban may prohibit vision of pictures of nude bodies as well as of

64 Plato, Politeia, 10th book, 596 a–598 d and Sophistes 235 b–236.

65 Gen. 2.17.

face-to-face vision of nude bodies. It might be interesting to investigate whether these prohibitions are of the same kind and to what extent they distinguish between the viewing of a depiction of an object and the viewing of the object depicted. In this respect, "law and images" borders a more general "law and vision", which not least is also indirectly addressed by "law and images" for the additional reason that pictures can both be depictions of something else and, at the same time, objects of their own.

Indeed, prohibitions relating to an image of an object and the object itself are often involved when it comes to prohibitions based on religious grounds, where the motivational strands for image prohibitions are generally more complex. For example, the Mosaic prohibition of images, which is mostly cited as the paradigm example of a ban on images, is by no means concerned with the harmfulness of the sight of the golden calf, but rather with the theologically problematic question of its use and instrumentalization for the worship of idols as false gods.[66] The core of the offence is the worship of the calf as deity, since it fundamentally questions Yahweh's monotheistic position. As is well known, in the 15th century, the Concilium Tridentinum, held between 1545 and 1563 in Trento, recognizing that images could well be useful for the transmission of faith, solved the problem by distinguishing between prohibited worship of images as idolatry on the one hand, and the permitted worship of the God depicted through, and with the help of the picture on the other hand. Admittedly, not all viewers of pictures adhered to this subtle distinction. Rather, from the iconoclastic movements from the Byzantine iconoclastic controversy ("eikonomachía"), the stripping of churches from their pictures in the name of the Protestant faith to the desecration of portraits and the contemporary dismantling of statues of overthrown rulers the wrath directed at the images intends to punish the physical images on behalf of the one for whom these images stand or the ideology they represent.[67] Even today, some legal image prohibitions aim at destroying the immaterial existence of images by attacking the physical embodiment, such as in cases in which the ban aims at preventing already the production of certain images or orders the destruction of physical copies thereof. Of course, in recent times some image prohibitions have been added which are not motivated by the harmfulness of the image in its effect on the viewer, but which are mainly concerned with the welfare and dignity of the people depicted. Examples are the prohibition of pornographic

---

66 For the different formulations of the mosaic picture ban see Ex. 20, 4, Dtn. 4, 16–18 and 5, 8.

67 Belting (1990/1997), pp. 166–7; Freedberg (1989), pp. 378 et seq.

depictions of children as well as the punishment of curious onlookers who take photographs of victims of traffic accidents.

In line with these different, partly interwoven motivations, image prohibitions are to be found in widely divergent areas of law such as criminal law (state security, but also pornography, etc.), civil law (especially copyright law, but also personal rights, laws against unfair competition, etc.) and public law (data protection, regulation of video surveillance in public spaces, etc.). In an increasingly visually oriented society, the issues addressed by these image regulations go well beyond the traditional prohibitions which mainly aim at protecting state secrecy interests and visual material considered to be of an indecent and pornographic nature or as glorifying violence. Today, additional issues regulated by law deal with the possibilities to control one's own (life) image by way of personality rights; the commercial exploitation of images by way of normatively secured possibilities of appropriation of "image" resources provided for mainly by copyright and, as far as imaging techniques are concerned, by patent law.[68] Those image prohibitions as well as legal rules regarding the creation, communication, trade and consumption of images intend to help stabilizing the social and economic order. To what extent, however, image prohibitions achieve the goal that they were initially designed for, and to what extent they are fundamentally suitable for this purpose, are questions that need to be examined in more detail by way of separate sector-specific case studies. Within such case studies it seems appropriate not only to ask about the efficiency of a particular prohibition, but to verify – as has been doubted in recent discussions about the harmful effects of ego-shooter games – whether the negative effect which the rule undertakes to prevent, does at all exist.

3.2 *Commandments*

In a mirror image way to normative prohibitions of images, which intend to keep a negative influence away from the observer and want to prevent the observer from seeing certain depictions which are considered as dangerous, pictorial commandments on the other hand aim at making the observer look at certain images, relying on a positive influence of the message transported by the pictures. In other words, if the behaviour of the potential viewer is to remain unchanged in the case of image prohibitions, it is to be altered in the case of image commandments. The road user should behave according to the

68 For systematic overviews according to German law see Wanckel (2017); Castendyk (2012); Hoeren/Nielen (2003); Koch (2003); for the history of patent law relating to photography see Dreier (2011) and (2019), pp. 213 et seq.

traffic signs, the addressee of a donation appeal should donate, and the viewer of an advertising poster should buy the product advertised.

As stated above, although image prohibitions and image commandments do not share a common belief in the detrimental or beneficial effects of images, they both proceed alike from the anthropologically conditioned attention reflex, which instinctively and with an automatically triggered reflex reacts to disturbances in the environmental pattern as perceived by the human eye. Image prohibitions aim at preventing the triggering of this reflex, whereas image commandments do all they can to stimulate it.

This apparently unbreakable power of images to attract the viewer's attention without his or her conscious will has prompted some authors of image theory to ascribe the active part in visual communication not to the observer, but to the picture which is seen as the true actor. According to this line of thinking, it is no longer the viewer who observes a picture. Rather, the picture is the subject which actively looks at the viewer. While in Elkins' work the picture only "stares back" in response to the human observer's gaze, Mitchell ascribes the images a "personhood" of their own in terms of what they "want". In Bredekamp's work, the image then becomes a largely independent subject in its entirety, not only reciprocating the human gaze, but also challenging the onlookers' reaction by way of what he calls "image acts" ("*Bildakte*").[69] Of course, in rejecting the traditional viewer's and hence anthropocentric perspective, this newer approach seems to continue the history of enlightenment and rational penetration. At the same time, however, the attribution to inanimate pictures of the ability to address an independent appeal to the viewer is as such more closely related to mysticism than to rationalism. As such, it rather looks like a fall back into natural religious ways of explaining the world, of which Mitchell is well aware of.[70] Attributing an active act to images merely transfers pre-modern animistic notions of nature onto images and hence on human artefacts. Just as the reason for animism of nature is the desire to tame the human fear of nature's uncontrollable phenomena by way of imputing to them a life of their own, legal prohibitions of images appear to be concerned with conjuring up and conquering the viewer's fear of the power and the inscrutable functional mechanism of the images banned.[71] In the times of ubiquitously installed surveillance cameras, however, it is indeed – if not

69 Elkins (1996), pp. 46 et seq.; Mitchell (2005), pp. 30 et seq.; Bredekamp (2010/2018), pp. 20 et seq.

70 Mitchell (2005), pp. 28–29 ("flirts with a regressive, superstitious attitude towards images, one that if taken seriously would return us to practices like totemism, fetishism, idolatry and animism").

71 Boehme-Neßler (2010), pp. 25–26, related, however, to oral cultures.

the images themselves, then certainly – the image-producing cameras that cast their gaze on the passers-by, constantly looking and recording the latter's movements and activities.

In one respect, however, commandments to look at images differ from image prohibitions. Whereas image prohibitions apply directly to those images, the creation and visibility of which is to be prevented, this is only partially true for image commandments, where such direct application is mainly to be found only when a legal norm orders the erection of a traffic sign. In addition, regarding their legal effect as administrative acts, traffic signs are self-enforcing. Apart from that, however, looking at images cannot as such be enforced. Rather, the image that is or wants to be seen can only operate successfully by triggering the attention reflex of the person in whose field of vision it appears. For this reason, the size of the images, the frequency of their presentation and the surprise caused by its content play an important role in the struggle for the increasingly scarce resource of attention and hence for the normative force that emanates of a certain image.

3.3 *Common Problems*

Despite all differences, image prohibitions and image commandments do meet some of the same challenges regarding the semantic interpretation by different viewers and the psychologic effects images have on them. These challenges have to do with the human perception of visual *stimuli* which, from a neuroscientific and cognitive-psychological perspective are to be described as the three stages of perception, processing and storage of visual information. To begin with, humans can only see what the human eye is capable of perceiving, the spectre of light waves between 380 and 780 nanometers, ranging from blue-violet to green and yellow to dark red. Likewise, it is known that perception is not a passive act and not an act of isomorphic depiction, but rather a multi-layered construction of the content of the visual information that has reached the eye. How a person interprets and understands the content of an image he or she sees largely depends on the memory of images that person has previously seen as well as on past experiences, attitudes and other predispositions of the respective viewer.[72] Although it may be assumed that images on the retina of the human eye are quite similar from one person to the other, it is yet unclear what the light stimulus on the retina of the eye triggers in the brain and how this is being done.[73] The ambiguity of the meaning of images has less

72 See, e.g., Goodman (1968/1976), p. 10, and, for a summary on psychological – both experiential and recognition-based – theories of depiction Hyman/Bantinaki (2017).

73 Summarizing, Boehme-Neßler (2010), pp. 63 et seq. with additional references.

to do with the blurriness of the images themselves than with the ambiguity of the processing of retinal signals in the brain of the person viewing the image. It is indeed a sobering finding that the effect of the images on viewers and hence their meaning will always remain a mystery and can at best be empirically ascertained.

It might be added that the issue is even more complex in the case of photography, where the viewer not only looks at a photographic depiction but where at the same time the viewer also gets a visual impression of the object depicted.[74] What the viewer "sees" is not only a picture and an image, but he also has the impression of looking "through" the photograph to the object depicted in the image which is presented in the form of a picture, as blurred, vague and distorted that depiction might be.[75] However, whereas in the case of painting it is clearly understood that the depiction is not identical in all its features with the object depicted, due to their apparent realism this is much less clear when it comes to looking at photographs. Although photography appears to present a truthful image of the object depicted, what the photograph shows depends to quite some extent not only on the technology used in order to make, develop – in digital technology replaced by the properties of the recording software – and print a photograph, but also on the choices made by the photographer and those persons who make use of a photograph for a certain purpose in a certain context. Photographs, it may be said, are therefore only partly a trace of the world, but to another extent an expression of the medium by means of which they are produced. In other words, although an indexical trace leads from the object depicted to its depiction on the photograph, the reverse cannot be said. This discrepancy is even more acute regarding digital photographs where the software used in between the taking and the storage as well as, ultimately, the projection defines what will be seen.[76] Finally, the possibilities of undetectable image manipulations and ultimately the construction of digital images which only look like depicting a real object make it even more difficult to understand what exactly a viewer sees when looking at an object that seems to show all the characteristics of a photograph and which is apparently truthful to the reality it shows.[77]

---

74 See above 2.1.

75 This has been described many times, see only, e.g., Walton (1984); critical towards the transparency claim even in the case of photographs, however, e.g., Currie (1995).

76 Belting (2001/2011), p. 144 of the English and p. 213 of the German edition, who by arguing against Barthes and invoking Sontag and Flusser generally denies these pictures the character of a "replica of the world".

77 For discussion, see below, 4.1.

These doubts about the human perception and interpretation of images have two important consequences for the regulation of images by law. Firstly, since the individual visual experience of one viewer cannot be directly compared with that of another viewer, the only possibility to discuss images is to achieve an intersubjective understanding concerning the content of images on the basis of what has been perceived. Secondly, the insecurity of what images mean to the individual viewers is the crucial point for any attempt to regulate images by way of either prohibitions or commandments. Because it is unclear whether the depiction accurately captures and whether the viewer accurately experiences what is relevant from the point of view of the prohibition while looking at a certain image, it is difficult for any image regulation to target the exact point of attachment. Comparable to a broad-spectrum antibiotic that works throughout the entire human body, every prohibition of images inevitably has certain scattering effects and can never be sure of sanctioning what it intends to sanction. Due to the vagueness of what they say, images appear to the lawmaker as a sort of a moving target, which both legal prohibitions and legal commandments can, if at all, only hit in part. In the case of legal prohibitions, either too little is forbidden or too much so that there always is a danger of over-blocking as well as of under-blocking. In addition, there always is the danger of "false positives" as well as "false negatives", especially when the enforcement of prohibitions is automated based on pre-defined algorithms, as it has become apparent in the case of the privatised control of images by platform operators. The problem is even more acute when it comes to image commandments where the norm giver can never be sure that the images presented to be looked at will be understood by the viewers in the way the images were intended by those showing them or in the way the norm giver understood them.

4 The Impact of Digitisation and Networking

Like any new technology, digitisation and distribution via the internet influence upon both our understanding and the communicative uses we make of images, as well as upon the legal rules which are intended to regulate the production, dissemination and use of images.

4.1 *Images and Digitisation*

Initially, the changes brought about for images by digitisation and networking have mostly caused fears. The resulting defensive reflexes themselves reflected in the colloquial designation of the multitude of images as a "flood of images". This term clearly indicates the "failure to cope with the leap to a new medium".[78] At the same time, it betrays a lack of pictorial competence in dealing with and the feeling of "powerlessness vis-à-vis and the defence" against the newly formatted images.[79] The associations evoked by the term "flood" refer to fears of a breach in the dam, of flooding, drowning, and ultimately the destruction of the auratic individual icons by a faceless, uniform mass of everyday images. Even the related, yet not identical term of "inflation of images" contains, as Wolfgang Ullrich has pointed out, at its core a complaint about the loss of value and hence of meaning of the individual image.[80]

Such fears are not limited to the public at large and the popular press. Also, parts of the image sciences and particularly the theory of photography reacted with extreme scepticism. The fact that – like analogue photography – digital photography also works with classical lenses did not prevent photo theorists from diagnosing an exceedingly radical confrontation of photography with electronic imaging technologies, and a radical break away from analogue photography.[81] In this view, the theoretically complete manipulability of digital photographs and the possibility of integrating digital pictorial material into a continuum of indexical, iconic, and symbolic images, gave rise to an ontological doubt, since it meant nothing less than a blurring if not a complete wiping out of the indexical trace that connects the visible image with the allegedly depicted object.[82] There was talk of a "black hole" that would sooner or later swallow up the photographic by way of digital image processing,[83] of the "end of photography"[84] and the "end of the photographic age"[85] as well as of "photography after photography"[86] or the beginning of a "post-photographic era".[87]

---

78 Vismann (2007), p. 21 (translation of the original German quotation by the author).

79 Bredekamp (2010/2018), p. 13.

80 Ullrich (2003), pp. 66 et seq.

81 In German literature, see, e.g., Lunenfeld (2010), p. 347; summarizing Geimer (2009), pp. 98 et seq.

82 See especially Mitchell (1992a); Stiegler (2010), pp. 22 and 339/340.

83 Lunenfeld (2010), p. 351.

84 Hockney, The Guardian of 4 March 2004 ("digital technology is ending the rule of the one-eyed monster that never lied"); https://www.theguardian.com/artanddesign/2004/mar/04/photography.

85 See the subtitle of the two volumes collecting theoretical essays on photography by Wolf (2002) und (2003).

86 Amelunxen/Iglhaut/Rötzer (1995).

87 Mitchell (1992a), p. 20.

However, all these predictions seem to overlook that the question of the authenticity of image was already an issue well before the emergence of digital and even analogue photography.[88] Moreover, the kind of critique of technology just mentioned suffers from the paradox – the formulation of which is attributed to digital pioneer and critical activist Jerome Lanier as well as to Bill Gates – according to which any assessment of the consequences of the effects of new technologies tends to underestimate short-term effects and over-estimate long-term consequences. At the same time, there is a general tendency to attach disproportionate importance to the currently most exciting innovations, as well as to grasp new phenomena based on merely mono-causal explanations. However, predictions of future developments which are based on mono-causal argumentation alone only extrapolate current developments without considering opposing forces and complex feedback loops in reaction to the initial development which often slow down its exponential development. Similarly, and more specifically related to the images and their modes of production, Vilém Flusser's understanding exerted a lasting impact on subsequent theoretical discussions, according to which not only digital images, but all technically produced images brought about a radical change to images that were manually created.[89]

On closer examination, however, it becomes apparent that the ontological difference between continuous and discrete tonal values, which Mitchell and others consider decisive, does not constitute a qualitative leap regarding any possible loss of image quality. Quite like digital photography, analogue photography does know certain losses of image quality which is due to the grain size of the negative and the photographic paper. Compared to these, digital photography shows even higher rates of resolution. If there are losses in accuracy of digital photography, such losses are less the result of the discrete character of the tonal values, but rather of subsequent acts of compression.[90]

At the same time, the considerably expanded possibilities of digital manipulation do not necessarily lead to a complete break with indexicality. On the one hand, the assertion of the "this-is-as-it-has-been" cannot even be upheld in a general way for analogue photographs in view of the possibilities provided for by retouching the original photograph and the montage of parts of the image. Some authors even deny the indexical relationship between the picture and

88 Belting (2005); Wortmann (2003).

89 Flusser (1984), pp. 13 et seq.; similarly, Belting (2001/2011), pp. 27/28 of the English and pp. 41/42 of the German edition.

90 Lunenfeld (2010), p. 350.

the depicted altogether[91] in view of the mostly ideological manipulation of the content of even analogue images through the selection of the motifs taken, the cropping and framing, and not least the context in which the images are presented. Therefore, on the other hand, the fragility of the indexicality and the far-reaching detachment of images from the origin of their production equally exist in the case of analogue and of digital photography. The change which is the result of the leap from analogue to digital photography is therefore more of a quantitative than of a qualitative nature.[92] Of course, it is true that in pre-digital times disturbances of the indexical trace by way of image manipulations were perceived rather as the exception than as the rule,[93] whereas in post-digital times they appear to be the rule rather than the exception.[94]

Despite this gradual change in the manipulability of photographic images, the belief of the viewer in the reality of what he sees as depicted in a photograph seems to persist in the digital age. Even against better knowledge the gap between belief and credibility is widening. In a way, digital photographic images are still trusted but the trust is situated at another level. Instead of trusting the credibility on the level of the image as created by the camera, the trust the viewer can place in images nowadays rather is a trust in those who stand in for the presentation of a particular image.[95] But even this is not really a new phenomenon, since every image shown invariably is the result of a number of selective choices made, from deciding which image to take as the one best representing the particular subject to be photographed, to the decision which image to communicate to the media. In other words, even if the doubt about the indexicality of the image seen no longer permits certainty, a sufficient degree of trust will be left in the source from which the visual communication originates or which it transmits in the form of a news channel, a blog or a personal message. "Soberly considered", digital technology "only adds yet another possibility of intervention to the existing ones".[96] It is therefore still a question

91 For such denial see the overview by Stiegler (2009) and van Gelder/Westgeest (2011).

92 On the detachment from production see Bruhn (2007); on the storage of generic image motifs by stock photography see Ullrich (2011b); and on the only quantitative difference between analogue and digital image Lunenfeld (2010), p. 350 ("shift of varying magnitude"). Burnett (2004) occupies a central position, seeing digital images located in the middle between object and subject; see also the texts in Wolf (2002), pp. 135 et seq.

93 On historically outstanding manipulations of images, see Haus der Geschichte (1989); on lies and deception in and through images Liebert/Metten (2007).

94 For a wide view of photo-fake see Weibel (2004), p. 66.

95 Similarly, Strauss (2003), pp. 71 et seq.; Wiedemann (2005) with proposals for safeguarding media trust, but still at a time before the appearance of "Social Bots" and "Fake News".

96 Stiegler (2010), p. 340.

not only of understanding images as constructions, but also of making reality as construction visible in the image.[97]

Likewise, continuity between analogue and digital can still be assumed if one makes a distinction between image production and picture design, according to which the material picture is to be distinguished from the immaterial image that appears in that material picture. Based on this distinction, images can be said to migrate and transcend the boundaries of different media and find their way from an earlier to a newer medium. In a similar way, the art historian Hans Belting sees a continuity of the different forms of representations of images which are all captured by his anthropological notion of "the image".[98]

In sum, digital photography does not mean the end of the production of images which depict reality. Yet, it has many effects in terms of image theory as well as regarding sociology and cultural history. This applies for one thing to the images themselves, which no longer appear in the singular, but rather in the plural.[99] Of course, the beginnings of this shift from the singular to the plural date back to older reproduction technologies. What is important, however, is that it is no longer just a few viewers who get into contact with a limited number of images, and it is no longer possible for everyone to view images only in specific sacred and non-sacred places intended specifically for this purpose. Moreover, although it is true that even a picture, which appears to be an indexical trace, is based less on a depiction of "what has at one point in time been at this place" than on a construction of the image shown, nowadays digital photography is characterized by a gradual transition from partly real, partly composed images to fully computer-constructed and elaborated graphics, by means of which virtual realities are constructed under the cloak of the real, and in which the trace of the "it has been like this" is ultimately lost. But even then, there still is some sort of anthropomorphic connection to mental images, pictorial ideas and pictorial designs of and by the person responsible for the creation of these non-indexical images.

From an image-scientific, sociological and physiological point of view, the additional question arises to what extent traditional images – particularly images of the characteristics that make up a human being – will be transformed. Digitally constructed representations of human beings may still differ in detail from real living beings. However, it is only a question of increased computing

97 Ibid., pp. 22/23.

98 Belting (2001/2011), pp. 1, 25 et seq. and 146 et seq. of the English and pp. 8, 38 et seq. and 218 et seq. of the German edition.

99 Ullrich (2003), pp. 66 et seq.; Ganz/Thürlemann (2010); Thürlemann (2013).

power and intelligent software that composite images can be created from several models, so that it is no longer possible to tell whether a real object is depicted or whether what looks like the depiction of a real object was created on, in and by a computer. It may well be true that almost realistic human representations seem to be more disturbing to viewers and trigger less empathy than less realistic representations.[100] Theoretically, however, no serious obstacle is discernible that would stand in the way of images generated by computer programs that can no longer be distinguished from real photographs. The viewer of what looks like a photographic image in the future can no longer be certain that a human being has caused the creation of this concrete image. In view of the intelligence distributed between man and machine, it will at the same time become more and more difficult to determine the author or authors of images who would be responsible for the image content.[101]

It is true that for the broad field of family, friend, party and event photography the technological difference between analogue and digital images is, in principle, irrelevant.[102] But it nevertheless has a decisive effect on the social use that is being made of images. The democratization of access to ever more powerful cameras now also supplied in smartphones, and above all the almost limitless storage space, no longer impose any restrictions on photographers in terms of the number of shots they can take. Driven by a merciless innovation competition, the technology defines and at the same time fulfils needs in relation to the images as soon as – and in many instances even before – the users have articulated them. The tremendous increase in the number of non-professional photographers is catered to by the perfection of the autofocus, the possibility of automatic continuous shooting and shooting in ever weaker light, by anti-shake protection and facial recognition including a multitude of other possibilities which previously were – if at all – only available to professional photographers. The postulate of the "end of photography" can therefore at best mean that whatever images meant in times of analogue photography has ceased to exist in its previous form. The images that are produced millions of times today and circulate in masses in individual communications as well as in social networks are images different from those that were known before. In other words, if we are talking about images today, then other objects are referred to than those that were meant almost half a century ago under the very same name. This phenomenon is indeed a notable parallel to the changed

100 On this perception-psychological valley called "uncanny valley" in the realism sympathy curve see Mori, M./MacDorman, K.F./Kageki, N. (2012).

101 For a detailed account see Burnett (2004).

102 Stiegler (2010), p. 105.

understanding of the work of art in the age of mechanical reproduction as diagnosed by Walter Benjamin in the first half of the 20th century.[103]

At the same time, the sharing of individual images has developed into an unprecedented form of visual communication, the full impact of which has yet to be discovered.[104] Of course, sharing in the form of one to many was already made possibly by television, but this did not enable the individual producer of images to share them. Via the internet, however, outside of closed user groups the sharing of images leads to a visibility that goes far beyond what could be perceived by the circulation of analogue images, since both in terms of speed and geographical distribution the latter was tied to the dissemination of a physical carrier medium. Also, there was a temporal limitation of visibility in the sense that to access an image of the past, a physical copy of it had to be retrieved from a book, a library or an archive. At the same time, it was clear that an image which was stored in a library, i.e. in one place, was taken at an earlier point in time. On the internet, however, which is accessible throughout the whole world, there is no such one place. Likewise, it is not immediately visible whether the image that shows up after an image search on the internet is an image of a current or of a past event. In digital networks, everything visible is equally accessible everywhere and at any time, far beyond what was possible by television. In as much as the internet doesn't know a "here" and "there", it also doesn't know a "now" and "then". This is of considerable importance for the ecology of individual and collective memory. In the analogue environment loss and forgetting were the rule, and preservation the exception. Hence, active efforts were called for to avoid the default rule of loss and forgetting. In contrast, in the digital environment preservation is the rule, and forgetting the exception, so that active efforts are called for in order to avoid the default rule of preserving.[105] It might be added that at the same time, it is not so much the technique of finding by powerful search engines that is the decisive factor in implementing strategies of preservation, but rather the statistics produced by searches in big data, which enable the person who undertakes the search to recognize patterns and not necessarily causalities, but mere correlations in the abundance of available text and image information.

The analysis of large amounts of data has a further consequence. In contrast to the analogous representation of an image, where it was clear what the entirety of the image was, digital images disintegrate into single pixels, which as

103 Benjamin (1937/1971–1989; similarly already before *Valéry*, Pièces sur l'art, Paris 1931 ("grandes nouveautés transforment toute la technique des arts … et aillent … jusqu'à merveilleusement modifier la notion même de l'art").

104 For an inventory see Gerling/Holschbach/Löffler (2017).

105 Mayer-Schönberger (2009).

such can be carriers of information. In other words, in the digital format the image the meaning of which was initially determined by the relationships between the individual image elements, is being fragmentized during the process of big data analysis into a multitude of pixels of equal value and unconnected meaning, which can be searched and re-assembled in any other form. The decisive question then is which criteria are to be used to combine individual pixels into an "image" or "images", as well as to ascertain the relationship between data, executing computer program, and image.[106] What is the representative and what is represented?

The digital artwork "unitape" by media artist Carsten Nicolai[107] is an excellent example of digital media art which illustrates the phenomenon just described. In a large-scale installation, graphic structures are projected onto a museum wall that recalls old punch cards from the early days of mechanical data processing. The projection seems to interact with acoustic signals and the coding is thus made optically visible and at the same time transformed into music. This may give the viewer the impression that the image controls the music or that the music is translated into the image. In truth, however, the programmed data set is the starting point for both its visual and acoustic representations. In other words, the data set appears as a representation of both the image and the music. However, taken the other way around both the visible image and the audible music then appear as representations of the data set. The artist himself seems to oscillate between both perspectives, when he describes his work as "encoding complex visual information in a digital language" and talks about the "acoustic signals ... being themselves initially produced in a computer".[108] Ultimately, however, the focus is no longer on the image or the music, but on the data set. Image and music only serve to illustrate – and represent – the data.[109]

It is precisely this reversal of the causal point of view, which characterizes the effects of the digital revolution on the different media, including text and images. At the centre are not images and/or text, but the data which rather than representing them are represented by the resulting text and image. If the viewer nevertheless still perceives the image or the music as the main object, this proves nothing more than how lastingly the description and perception of images and their media representations are shaped by historical experiences

106 For additional discussion see Nake (2005); already earlier on the question of the art character of computer-generated images Franke (1987) and Steller (1992); on the connection between artwork and computer Müller (1987); see also Schirra (2005), as well as the contributions in Sachs-Hombach (2005a), pp. 494 et seq.

107 Carsten Nicolai, unitape, www.carstennicolai.de/?c=works&w=unitape.

108 Ibid.

109 Keyif/Korintenberg/Zhang (2017).

and viewing habits. Only because the images were first in the world as physical, analogue objects did the understanding of the data set as a representation of the image and the music emerge, just as the notation represents music which according to an idealistic understanding of the world, is as such thought of as existing outside of the notation. In the digital environment, however, "all these elements are merely different manifestations of the data stored in binary form".[110]

Of course, it could be argued that the image must first be implemented in the data set before it can be made visible based on these data. However, such an attempt to preserve the traditional anthropomorphic understanding of the image loses its power of persuasion once the images will be devised by autonomous, self-learning digital devices. Digital surveillance cameras are a good example, where the link between the autonomous system and the human being who designed and installed the system is severed to the extent to which these systems "decide" themselves who, what, at what time and in which situation will be looked at and recorded. The old fear of the power of the images we look at transforms itself into a new fear nourished by the fact that the passer-by does not know which images are being taken at which point in time and, above all, who will be looking at the images taken or how they will be automatically processed. It will therefore be the task of the law to protect against this new fear by rules concerning the responsibility of those who design these systems and who make use of such autonomously generated images. Moreover, the link to human pre-images comes to an end with digital images created based on applications that make use of artificial intelligence. The bond between the object and the interpretation determined from it by means of a visual intermediate step is severed once data are no longer made visible for the human eye according to criteria which can no longer be fully understood but are primarily used for automatic data processing performed to come up with suggestions for the resulting human behaviour.

Finally, it should only briefly be mentioned that digital images – apart from their appearance also as moving images which are not particularly addressed here – have already begun to venture from the second into the third dimension in the form of augmented and completely virtual reality (AR and VR). Whereas AR, i.e. virtual additions to the real environment by additional content, as well as mixed realities (MR), i.e. the replacement of real objects by virtual objects or the modification of real objects by virtual changes are located on the borderline between two- and three-dimensionality, VR re-positions the viewer from a position *in front of* the image to a position *within*

110 Lunenfeld (2010), S. 351.

the image. Reversing the earlier reduction of the three-dimensional real space to the two-dimensional surface of the canvas as the material support of the image, VR deceives the viewers' senses into believing in what is no more than a deceptively real reality. It has been said that contrary to the initial reduction from three dimensions to two dimensions, which eliminated the third dimension of space and hence gravity, thus allowing for representations without weight, idealistic speculation and pure thought, the adding of a virtual and hence deceptive third dimension does not re-establish gravity, but rather also allows for weightlessness.[111] Be that as it may, just as the history of surveillance cameras has fundamentally changed the understanding of what constitutes reality through distance vision, so too will the further development of these techniques profoundly change expectations of the composition, truthfulness and meaning of images.

Summing up, it can be concluded that depending on the perspective taken, "in the age of digitalization almost everything or almost nothing has changed".[112] However, since explaining what is new always has to be set in relation to what is already known from the past, it is not surprising that even today the term "digital photography" still makes reference to "photography", thus emphasizing the continuity of photography in the digital image with a view to the present and the future. At the same time, "digital photography" also refers to the discontinuity of digital photography in comparison to analogue photography. Similarly, one still speaks of the digital image recording device as a "camera", even in cases where the camera no longer exists as an independent apparatus, but where its function is integrated into other devices such as smartphones and tablets. It is hardly surprising that this function is mostly still symbolized by an icon in the form of a stylized traditional camera. Sometimes one can even find technically outdated features such as the lever for selecting the aperture or for removing the bayonet catch of the lens, the viewfinder window and the housing structure necessary for holding the reflex mirror (Fig. 2).

4.2 *Digitisation and the Law*

Just like images, the law also sees itself confronted with the challenges of digitisation and networking. These challenges address different problem areas.[113]

---

111 Sloterdijk (2018), pp. 49 et seq.

112 Geimer (2009), pp. 104–105 (translation of the original German quotation by the author).

113 For detailed accounts of the legal changes provoked by digitization and networking technologies, see in English literature Michalos (2004) and in German legal literature Herbort (2017).

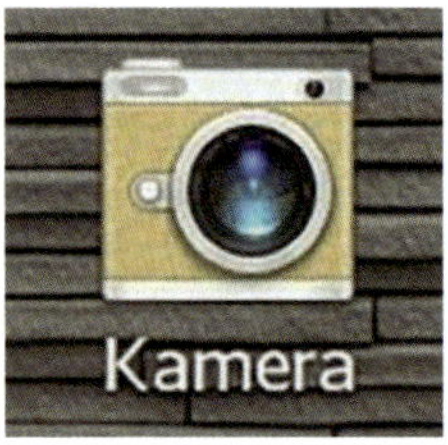

FIGURE 2
"Camera"-icon shown on the display of a smartphone (2014)

With regard to copyright, in the beginning the legal discussion centred on the change which made it possible, contrary to works in analogue form, to reproduce digitally formatted works including images, without loss of quality and at marginal cost, i.e. at the mere cost of copying.[114] Since potential users no longer had to purchase a copy of the protected work from the producer, right-holders feared an erosion of the economic value of their rights to distribute analogue copies and the business models based upon thereon. This development was aggravated by the use of the technology developed by computer scientists for direct information transfer between individual private nodes on the network (so-called peer-to-peer file sharing). Both phenomena – ease of copying and ease of communication – severely limited the control of the original manufacturers' distribution of their content.

As a reaction, according to the slogan "The answer to the machine is in the machine"[115] right holders sought to defend themselves mainly by means of digital watermarks and similar identification markings, but increasingly also by way of technical protection mechanisms designed to control both access to, and the kind of uses to be made of copyrighted works. Since initially not all these technical means proved to be successful, right holders convinced the legislature to extend existing copyright protection by way of granting, on top of copyright, an additional legal protection scheme against the unauthorised circumvention of technical protection measures. This anti-circumvention protection includes protection against "the manufacture, import, distribution, sale, rental, advertisement for sale or rental, or possession for commercial purposes of devices, products or components or the provision of services which have only a limited commercially significant purpose or use other than to circumvent, or which are primarily designed, produced, adapted or performed for the purpose of enabling or facilitating the circumvention of technological

114 For an early account see Dreier/Becker (1994).
115 Clark (1996).

protection measures".[116] In addition, a few years later, the manufacturers were also able to rely on streaming technology, product keys, and technical encapsulations of the content, thus excluding users to a considerable extent from direct access to the data representing the content.

As already described at the turn of the millennium by Jeremy Rifkin, this development results in a paradigm shift from "having", i.e. owning, copies of works on the basis of a property right, towards mere "access", i.e. using a protected work on the basis of a temporary permission.[117] In addition, both in the proprietary and the open content-worlds the collective public enjoyment of protected works is replaced by a star-shaped connection which links each individual user directly to the provider who is therefore able to exactly control how much access will be granted to each individual user. Hence, social networking platforms notwithstanding, the networked freedom of the internet transforms itself into the social isolation of the individuals which consume copyrighted – and, by the way also non-copyrighted – material.[118] At the same time, digitization and networking result in a transformation of products into services, which enable producers to tailor their customers' possible uses to suit their own profit motives, irrespective of which balance between ownership and access interests has been legally prescribed by the lawmaker.[119] This development, which can be characterized as private legislation and as "code as law", exclusively follows the laws of the market, externalizing non-economic public welfare interests.[120] Although its formation may still only be in the beginning, it will, however, no doubt continue rapidly the more of services on a digital basis will be moved to the cloud.

Of course, in terms of regulation theory, the private nature of what consumers are conceded to be able to do with regard to technically configured objects might not attract criticism as long as none of the competing providers of services of a certain kind have an exclusive monopoly and as long as a dominant market position is not abused to seek and obtain monopolistic rents and consumers are left with sufficient switching opportunities. However, this condition seems hardly to be fulfilled in view of the current oligopolistic

---

116 Art. 6 (1) and (2) of EU-Directive 2001/29/EC on Copyright in the Information Society, OJ L 176 of 22 June 2001, pp. 10 et seq.; see also Sec. 1201 of the US Copyright Act, Title 17 U.S.C. as amended by the Digital Millennium Copyright Act (DCMA) of 1998.

117 Rifkin (2000).

118 Houkes (2018).

119 For a detailed analysis, see Wielsch (2008); Specht (2019).

120 See, in particular, Samuelson (2003); Lessig (1999). This is, of course, altogether different in states in which political ideology rather than market forces is the decisive criterion for decision making.

structures that have presently developed in the market for platform and other Internet services. In addition, it is not to be overlooked that the functioning of the market is hampered, and competition distorted, by network effects (the more participants make use of the same system, the greater is this system's benefit to the individual participant), as well as by lock-in effects (the costs of switching to a new system are greater than the gains resulting from the use of a better offer from another provider).

How can the law react to these changes? The options available might be different for the legislature on the one hand, and the courts on the other.

The legislator may not yet have completely given out of his hands the possibility of controlling the behaviour of private image and service providers, even if the political scope for action is limited. Firstly, as a rule, legislation invariably lags behind the technological development that it intends to regulate.[121] Moreover, the legislator's room for manoeuvre in the field of the digital and its economic and social consequences faces the difficulty of having to deal with an increasing degree of differentiation of products, services and distribution models which make the legislator face a dilemma. Either the legislator votes for an ex-ante regulation that focuses on mostly uncertain forecasts of technological, economic, social and cultural developments. Choosing this option entails the risk of criticism and the accusation of being paternalistic as well as hostile to innovation. The other possibility for the legislator is to opt for ex-post regulation. However, in choosing this option, the legislator risks coming too late, since by the time legislation has passed all parliamentary hurdles the need for regulation may have already disappeared, or, in the worst case, the results of the technological change may no longer need to be corrected. The latter approach – and the risks that come with it – is generally opted for in the USA, which have a cultural tendency to give priority to a person's freedom to act and provide for drastic sanctions in the form of damages, if the acts committed prove to have been harmful to third parties. In Europe, in contrast, the inclination to grant injunctive relief, and especially preliminary injunctive relief against acts that might cause harm, is much greater, in particular in order to protect against potential hazards once a new technology emerges. In both jurisdictions, however, the developments just outlined leave the legislator little choice but to dispense with detailed regulations and confine itself to framework legislation. This, however, risks frustrating the expectations of legal certainty on the part of norm addressees and those subject to the norm.

121 Loewenheim, in: Schricker/Loewenheim (2017), Introduction, margin number 3 ("process of legal reaction to the challenges of technology and the resulting economic and societal developments"; translation of the original German quotation by the author).

At the same time, this opens the door for a migration of genuinely state decision-making tasks to the private sector, so that in individual cases such as regards images, it is no longer the state and its authorities deciding which im ages may be posted and which must be deleted, but rather major private players such as Google and Facebook, who are subject to only minor control and transparency obligations, if any at all.[122]

The courts for their part are closely bound to the wording of existing statutes according to the constitutional principle that binds the courts to the law.[123] In a deliberate departure from the "unlimited interpretation" under National Socialist rule,[124] the German courts endeavour to ensure that the interpretation is as unimpaired as possible by the "Zeitgeist". At the same time, this prevents them in some cases, without action on the part of the legislature, from taking due account of the rapid consequences of technological change. Especially in countries following the Roman legal tradition, one often encounters an almost scholastic interpretation of terms that originate from the analogue environment when they are applied to digital facts. The same is true, by the way, also in the countries of the Common Law legal system, insofar as detailed legal regulation excludes the courts from finding new solutions by way of "distinguishing" the new case at bar from previously decided cases. A prime example in this respect is the interpretation of the notion of "reproduction", one of the central concepts of national as well as international copyright law. This definition is comparatively clearly outlined as "tokens" of a work as far as analogue printed copies are concerned.[125] However, when abstracted from the printing process and transferred to the processes that occur in the course of electronic data processing, the transmission of an image and its viewing is miraculously accompanied by a whole multitude of "reproductions", from the scan of the original to the storage in the memory of the sending device, via the intermediate storage of the data in network routers lasting only milliseconds to the copies in the working memory, on the hard disk and possibly

122 On the right to be forgotten see CJEU, case C-131/12 of 13 May 2014 – Google Spain and Google. On the deliberate engagement of the major private players by the state see, e.g., § 3 of the German Act to Improve Law Enforcement in Social Networks (Network Enforcement Act) – NetzDG, Official Journal (BGBl.) I of 1 September 2017, pp. 3352 et seq.

123 In German law, see Article 20 (3) 2nd half-sentence of the German Fundamental Law (*Grundgesetz*).

124 See Rüthers (1973).

125 See, e.g., the entries "Vervielfältigung", "Token" and "Kopie" in Ortland/Dreier/Schmücker (forthcoming).

even during viewing on the screen.[126] Obviously, such interpretation does not take into account that in view of their partly ancillary function to the transmission and consumption of one and the same copyrighted work, many of them don't fulfil the economic and communicative functions that were traditionally fulfilled by an analogue copy. The courts are faced with similar problems when it comes to new forms of "distribution" and dissemination of images. It took the courts some time to pigeonhole the different forms of linking to someone else's copyrighted material into the existing system of exclusive rights, striking a highly differentiated balance between proprietary and access rights, which cannot be discussed here in detail.[127]

Of course, such an extension of the exclusive copyright protection extends the right holders' legal control powers far into the area of private uses about which the right holders are rather happy. Contrary to the analogue world, where the viewing of an image was copyright free, in the digital world the comparative process of equivalent communicative value is now subject to the control of the owner of the image rights and is therefore dependent on his consent. In other words, the proprietary sphere has been greatly extended to the detriment of the private sphere in which access was not controlled by the right holders. Here, to some extent, all too restrictive use conditions (end-user licensing agreements) may be subject to a control of standard terms and conditions. However, in recent times the courts rather abstain from interfering with market developments and newly developed business models which lead to a differentiation of products and services and which, as such, are generally considered as being for the benefit of consumers. Nevertheless, the problem remains that the current legal description of an object (the image) to which a subject (a holder of rights) has exclusive rights is at odds with the changes to be observed in the use of images in digital and networked communication. Here, the communication of one's own as well as someone else's images is not only about the actions of passing on the image as a tradable object. Rather, as

126 Paradigmatically CJEU, case C-5/08 of 16 July 2009 – Infopaq International. Differently before the enactment of the European Directive the German Federal Supreme Court (Bundesgerichtshof, BGH) of 4 October 1990, GRUR 1991, 449, 453 – Betriebssystem (technical acts of reproduction not necessarily seen as reproductions acts for purposes of copyright law).

127 See CJEU cases C-466/12 of 13 February 2004, ECLI:EU:C:2014:76 – Svensson (hyperlinking to freely available material originally posted with the consent of the right holder as free of copyright; C-348/13 of 21 October 2014, ECLI:EU:C:2014:2315 – BestWater (framing also copyright free) and C-160/15 of 8 September 2016, ECLI:EU:C:2016:644 – GS Media (linking to freely available material posted on the net without the consent of the right holder as a violation if copyright in case of knowing or having to know about the lack of consent).

can be seen on platforms such as Instagram, images are being used for purposes of self-representation and identity-finding, in an attempt to define the self-image through pictures taken by someone else and to gain self-confidence from recognition by way of the so-called "likes".

Finally, both legislation and jurisprudence are confronted with the fundamental change in the social conditions of the use of images. It is, of course, first of all a matter of the mass of mainly private images that becomes a problem, above all for the procedural processing of individual violations of the law, in the course of which the "great symbol machine of law" may indeed have served its purpose.[128] Moreover, the exponential increase in cameras installed in public places of both Western democracies and totalitarian states – purportedly for purposes of security of the citizens in one case, and for their outright control in the other case – likewise exercises normative control.[129] Above all, a fundamental shift and redefinition of the public and the private spheres can be seen. The borderline between these two spheres has shifted – albeit not exclusively, but nevertheless to a large extent – due to and in view of the digitization, networking and democratization of image-producing and image-communicating apparatuses. The resulting change affects both the horizontal demarcation of different groups of the public as well as the vertical demarcation line between the public and the private spheres.

Initially, the one monolithic public sphere with its noble and subsequently bourgeois concept of honour made a claim to political, social and cultural universality. The subsequent disintegration of this monolithic public sphere into a multitude of highly differentiated sub- and sub-sub-publics or "societies of individuals"[130] can be traced as far back as to the anti-bourgeois alternative social utopias designed before the First World War. Intensified by the youth movements of the 50s and 60s of the last century nowadays the partial public spheres each follow different rules which they have given themselves and whose formulation represents the decisive internal criterion for the constitution of the respective group as a sub-public which is outwardly differentiated from all the other groups. In the 80s of the 20th century, the introduction of private television then resulted, for the first time, in the demonstration and propagation of alternative lifestyles to a wider public. Finally, the democratization of the means of communication, triggered by innovative technological leaps in the form of the invention of the personal computer, the internet

---

128 Vismann (2007), p. 22.

129 See only Hempel/Metelmann (2005); Gaycken/Kurz (2008); Kammerer (2008); Bauman/Lyon (2012).

130 Sloterdijk (2004) ("*Individualgesellschaften*").

and, as regards images, of smartphones and social networking platforms, has fragmented what was once a unique and uniform public sphere even further into a multitude of sub-publics which all follow their different internal rules which include their own definitions of which form of communication is to be considered as public and which as private. For the time being, it is not possible to discern what counterforces between these sub-publics – some of which are hermetically sealed off from one another – could deploy sufficient social cohesion. At the same time, this atomization of the once monolithic public sphere is accompanied by an expectation of the individual to see his individuality upheld even in the public sphere, while letting into the private sphere what was formerly considered to be a public matter. Formerly private persons project their private lives into what used to be the public sphere, whereas public figures are in need of protecting their private lives as being dragged before the eyes of the public by paparazzi and the yellow press.[131] In this way, posts of images on social networking platforms that can be viewed publicly are often understood by those who post them as private self-portrayals, just as they claim the existence of a kind of cocoon of privacy around their body when they move around in public spaces which shall protect them against the intrusive views of photographers.[132] According to the German jurist Ladeur, this development – which goes hand in hand with the privatization of public spaces, transforming formerly freely accessible marketplaces into privately organized shopping malls[133] – means that "not only the idea of the function of the public sphere, but also the constitution of personality and the right to personality depend on processes of self-change in society and its reflection in public spaces."[134]

In sum, the informative and aesthetic expectations that viewers place on the images have changed, as has the way in which they are used to process

131 On stars and celebrities see Keller (2008); Schneider (2004); on the processing of problems by the legal institutions Steinhauer (2009); on paparazzi the exhibition catalogue edited by Chéroux (2014).

132 See, especially Nagel (2002), pp. 3 et seq.; Sofsky (2007); Rössler (2001); sceptical about the continued existence of the private sphere Schaar (2007); pleading for a voluntary abandoning of privacy, however, Heller (2011).

133 It should be noted that contrary to the USA, which is more open to the tendencies of propertising formerly public spaces, the German Constitutional Court has barred property owners of places that substitute for a public place from exercising their property rights in an all to broad way; see German Constitutional Court (Bundesverfassungsgericht) of 22 Febriary 2011, 1 BvR 699/06 – Fraport, and of 11 April 2018, 1 BvR 3080/09 – Stadionverbot.

134 Ladeur (2007), p. 55 (translation of the original German quotation by the author). – Fundamental from the point of view of sociology even before digitization and networking Sennett (1974).

information within the framework of social negotiation. In line with these changes the informative and aesthetic expectations that viewers place on the images have also undergone certain changes as have the ways in which images are used to process information within the framework of social negotiation.[135]

How did the law react to these changes?

As once again Ladeur has accurately described it, e.g. in Germany both the Federal Constitutional Court and the Federal Supreme Court have sought to react by developing an increasingly differentiated mechanism of balancing the conflicting individual fundamental rights of privacy on the one hand, against the freedom of information and of the press as well as artistic freedom all of which are also protected by the constitution, on the other. By attaching great importance to the freedom of expression in this weighing of conflicting constitutional rights, post-war German jurisprudence has indeed mastered the transition from a pre-democratic understanding of the public, based on socially recognised, extra-legal standards of conduct, to an understanding of the public as a forum for democratic discourse for the formation of opinion. However, so far the judiciary does not seem to have adequately reacted to the postmodern understanding of the public sphere with its numerous differentiated expectations regarding the safeguarding of individual validity claims that was initiated by the recent changes brought about by digitisation and networking. In response to this challenge, Ladeur postulates that "the services that the legal system can provide to maintain the self-renewal capacity of the social sub-sectors must not be thought of as a given 'task', assumed to be stable, or even from the point of view of the state, but must be prepared for change." In his view, the law should be more focusing on "observing patterns of order and rules of linkage in other sub-systems and on following them with its own rules, instead of making interests compatible with each other on a case-by-case basis."[136] The point is well taken, but it is yet difficult to see how such links to sub-systems other than the legal one could be established in court practice. Especially, interpreting existing legal rules in consideration of extra-legal social standards of conduct invariably runs the risk of giving in to the "Zeitgeist", thus opening the very flank which the institution of the law is intended to close, i.e. to keep the solution of an individual litigation free from actual extra-legal power relationships and ethical beliefs of the parties involved. Of course, the law can neither

135 See, e.g., Ullrich (1997); summarising Geimer (2009), pp. 106 et seq.; Lunenfeld (2010), pp. 347 et seq.

136 Ladeur (2007), pp. 42 and 276 (translation of the original German quotation by the author).

be immunised against the reality of life to be regulated, nor totally aligned with the respective trends of social behaviour. However, the courts do not act in a complete vacuum, sealed off from society and socially accepted patterns of behaviour, when they balance conflicting fundamental rights' positions. Rather, by repeatedly referring to a series of established values such as above all privacy, youth and data protection, which have become the cornerstones of the legal order via national and European fundamental rights, the courts are indeed capable of formulating adequate responses to changed circumstances and problems in a rather cautious way. Such an approach is perfectly suited to stabilising the legitimate expectations of the legal addressees regarding the plannability of their actions. At the same time, the repeated balancing of the rights in question enables the courts to gradually update and interpret statutory texts in the light of changing technical, economic and societal circumstances.

5 Images in Law, of Law, and for Law

As already noted in the introduction, the restraint of the law towards pictures doesn't exclude that besides the occasional images *in* law, a great number of images *of* law and legal actions has been created, which is increasingly complemented images that are created *for* the proper functioning of the law.[137]

5.1 *Images in Law*

Images of the first of the three categories just named, i.e. images *in* law, are to be found in legal norms, such as most notably traffic signs, but also signs containing age rating information of movies and computer games (Fig. 3) as well as in documents which contain legally relevant information, most notably technical drawings in patent applications and reproductions of protected trademarks and designs in the registers kept by patent and trademark offices (Fig. 4).[138] As noted above,[139] images in legal norms are to be found mainly in the image commandments, in which the pictorial sign is intended to induce the norm addressee to behave in a certain way, symbolized by the sign and described in more detail in the text of the law.

137 For a summary account of images in law and of law see in German literature, Röhl (2005).

138 Sachs-Hombach (2015 b), p. 174. On drawings in the European patent system see Rules 46, 48 and 49 of the Implementing Regulations to the European Patent Convention, as well as Parts A-IX and F-II,5 of the Guidelines for Examination.

139 See 3.2.

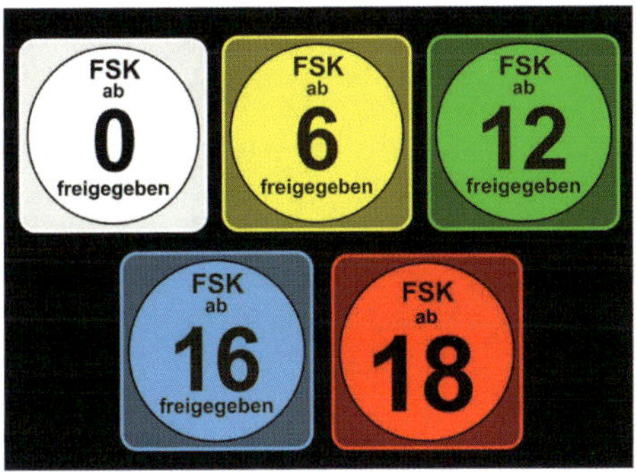

FIGURE 3
Age restriction symbols of the German Voluntary Self-Regulation Body of the Film Industry (Freiwillige Selbstkontrolle der Filmwirtschaft, FSK)

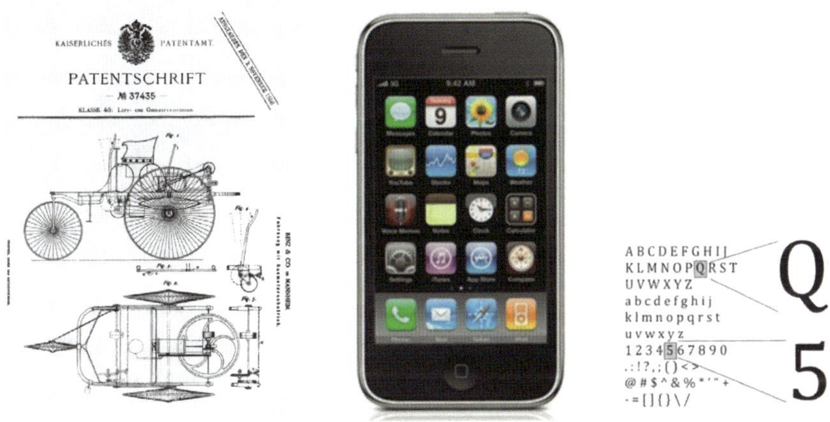

FIGURE 4 Examples of images from patent, design and type face protection registers.

Related are warning signs which come also in the form of traffic signs, but which may also consist in the mere mandatory representation of an image to the consumer, such as in the case of the health hazard photographs that must be shown on cigarette packets on the assumption that they might have a dissuasive effect on smokers (Fig. 5).

For some time, likewise private individuals, who derive their legal authority to set standards from their property and domestic law, have also been following the symbolic language of the legal traffic signs with the aim of regulating the behaviour of their increasingly international visitors (Fig. 6). Hence, a sign language that can be understood across language boundaries is developed that proves superior to multilingual verbalization and spelling out of the respective prohibitions.

In addition, as is demonstrated by the Creative Commons system, which visualises standardized licensing terms and conditions (Fig. 7), icons can be

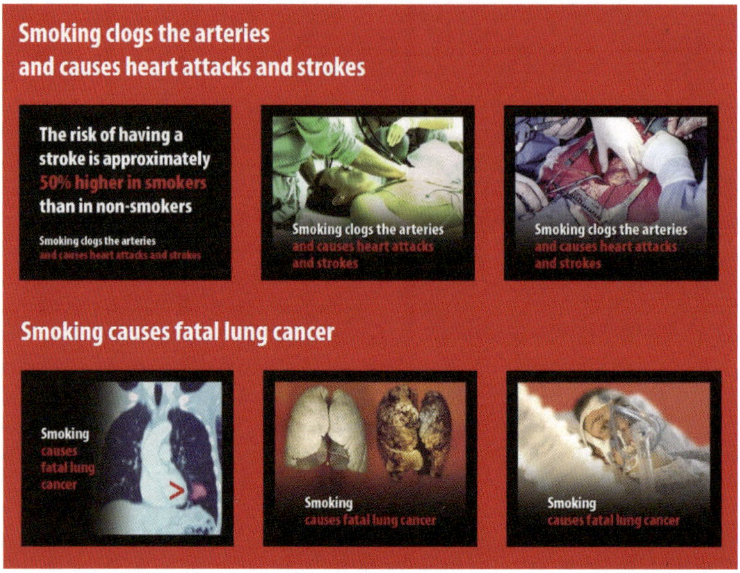

FIGURE 5 EU smoking warning signs (2005)

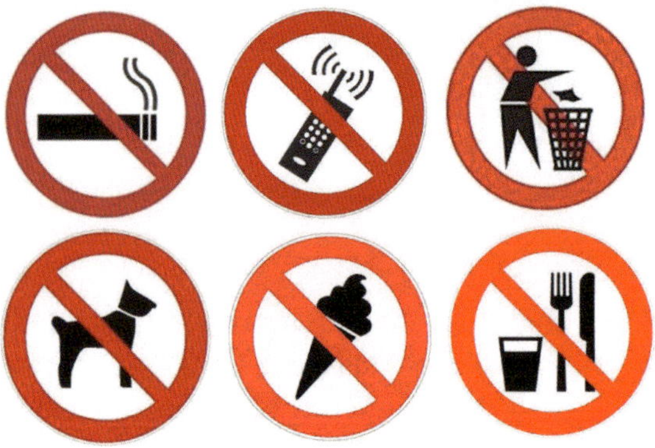

FIGURE 6 Private signs indicating prohibited behaviour

FIGURE 7 Creative Commons (CC) icons

used that symbolically refer to complex contractual clauses and make their core content visible and understandable at a glance.

Finally, it seems worth mentioning that many of these signs and icons find their way into legal documents and legal pleadings, where they join other pictorial material used for evidentiary purposes. However, most of these images remain in the files of the courts or the archives of clients and attorneys, unless they exceptionally find their way into publicly accessible court reports, which only happens when the image is needed to understand the argumentation of the court and the outcome of the case, such as often in patent, trademark, design and, to a limited extent, also in copyright cases.

5.2 *Images of Law*

The extensive corpus of images *of* law performs a whole series of different functions, which can provisionally be classified into the sub-categories of representation at a distance through visualization, of pictorial representations of law as an institution, of classical legal symbols and current symbolism of law, of schematic representations in law, of visual representations of legal actions and of forms of staged representations of the law. What all those sub-categories have in common is that they are intended to construct and "to convey certain beliefs and attitudes about the law".[140]

5.2.1 Representation at a Distance through Visualization

The first group of images of law, which in normative terms is the most powerful one, can be made out in the early portraits of emperors, as they had been standardized in the Roman Empire, especially since Emperor Augustus. The aim of these images was to ensure the emperor's presence throughout the empire. Not dissimilar to today's strategies of attracting attention, these images may had the purpose of propagating the fame of the emperor in a symbolized form, with the aim of keeping the emperor's presence alive in the memory of the subjects he was governing. Above all, however, it was a matter of symbolizing the claim to dominion, which was confirmed by issuing and by the authenticity of the coins which was in turn guaranteed by the portrait itself.[141]

Of greater normative importance were, of course, statues of and standards representing the Emperor, in front of which Roman soldiers performed sacrificial acts. One such example can be seen on a wall painting from Dura Europos around the year 230 (Fig. 8). In this ritual context, the image of the emperor

140 Sachs-Hombach (2005c), p. 174 (translation of the original German quotation by the author); Andina (2017).

141 Wohlfeil (2011).

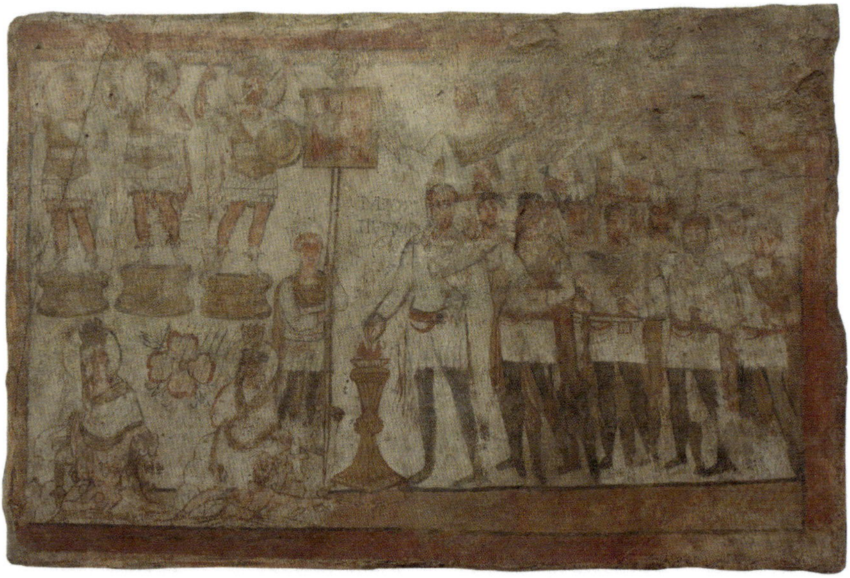

FIGURE 8 Sacrifice by Roman soldiers in front of imperial statues, mural painting, Dura Europos, ca. 230

was not only shown, but it represented the physically absent emperor in a legally binding manner as if he himself were present.[142] The late medieval effigy also belongs in this context, "which upholds the symbol of power after the death of the ruler and thus guarantees the continuity of state power through the image of the dead king".[143] Of course, even if a legal text enabled a more extensive rule of the land, the use of an image was better suited to fulfil the function that otherwise only came to written legal norms.

Still under the Roman emperors, the representative function of the imperial image changed to the form of the free-standing equestrian statue. The iconographic model of the equestrian statue of Mark Aurelius in Rome was subsequently – albeit only after a longer period of absence – resumed in the Middle Ages and in some isolated cases in Italian city-states. From then onwards, the freestanding equestrian statue of the French king Louis XIV in Paris represents the basic model of a form of representation of the respective ruler for all comparable statues, which spread rapidly in the European baroque

142 On the connection of Emperor and Deity see Rouge-Ducos (2011).

143 Joly, in: Joly/Vismann/Weitin (2007), S. 10; on the hypothesis of the effigies as the third body of the king beyond the "body natural" and the "body politic" see Marek (2007), pp. 56 et seq.

cities, if only largely stripped of its normative function. With a strongly weakened normative effect, the motif of the image of the emperor survived for a long time on coins, stamps and portraits of rulers in official offices. Especially in dictatorial states the image of the leader publicly displayed not only serves as a larger-than-life memento to those governed, but likewise manifests in his unique position the respective rulers claim to presence and autocracy.[144]

5.2.2 Pictorial Representations of Law as an Institution

A historically rather singular hybrid form, which can on the one hand be classified as images *of* law, but likewise, because of the juxtaposition of images to the legal text as images *in* law, are the illustrations of medieval legal texts, which can be found in the legal books such as the Sachsenspiegel of Eike von Repgow which was compiled between 1220 and 1235 (Fig. 9).

Unlike the miniatures with which the medieval copyists often ornate religious copies, the main purpose of these illustrations was to visually explain the content of the text to legal addressees who could not or not properly read. These private records of the law were no longer marked by the reticence towards images due to the Mosaic ban on images, which in those days was still evident in the copies of religious texts. Rather, text and image were combined in a completely purposeful rational way. Of course, at that time one could already refer to religious authorities, since Pope Gregory I (590–604) had advised with the propagation of a pragmatic image catechism to allow holy images with the aim of making the concepts of faith accessible and comprehensible to the illiterate among the faithful, who at that time constituted by far the majority of Christianity. However, in such visual representations of biblical as well as legal texts, priority was given to the written text and not to its pictorial representation in line with the beginning of the Gospel of John "in the beginning was the word".

5.2.3 Classical Legal Symbols

Following, images visualizing the content of the law withdrew to this very day. They were replaced by the symbolic visualization and representation of law as such as well as by symbols for legal institutions. Like any symbolic representation of abstract concepts and meanings, the symbolization of law also seeks to make the highly abstract idea of law and the internal logic of legal norms and their narrative structure understandable by pictorial means. According to the internal mechanism of symbols, this does not necessarily require a depiction

144 For the functional equivalent of commercial billboard advertising in democratic capitalist societies see Dreier (2019), pp. 248 et seq.

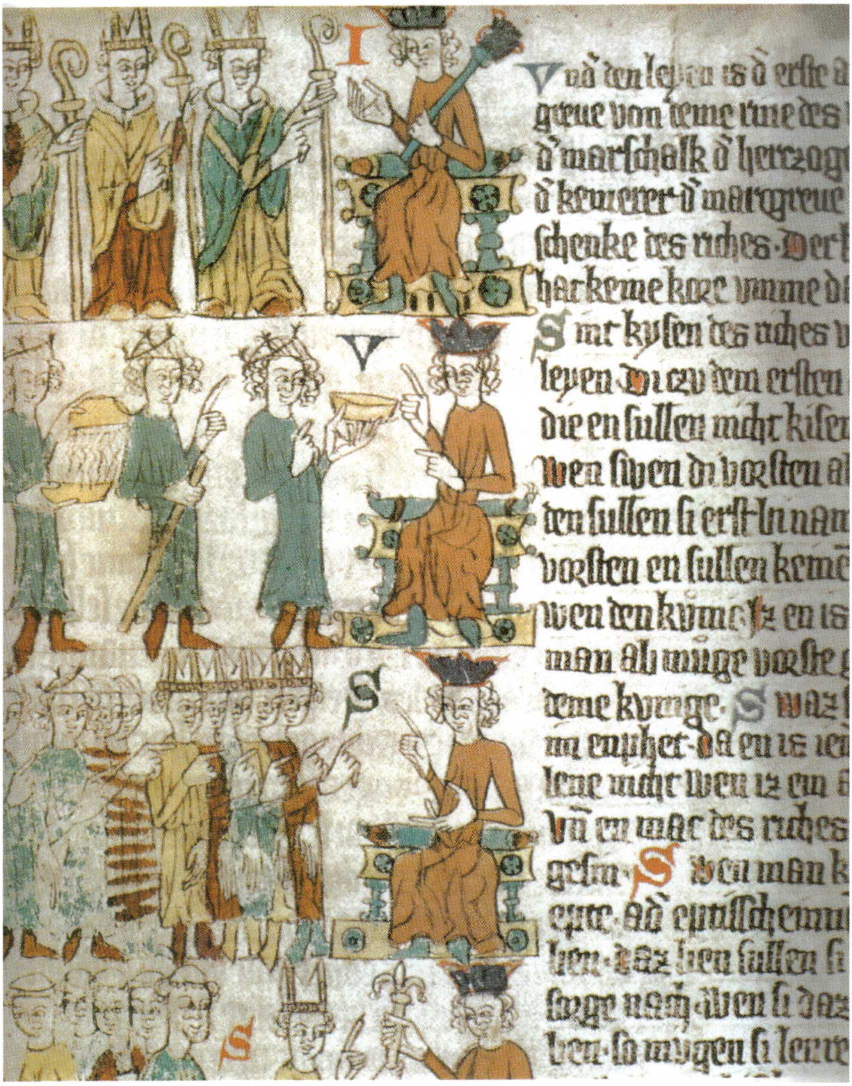

FIGURE 9 Eike von Repgow, Representation of the election of the king, Heidelberger Sachsenspiegel (Cod. Pal. Germ. 164, 21 r) (ca. 1300)

of legally relevant facts or regulatory contexts. Rather, any image and any sign may, in theory, serve as a symbol, provided it is understood by its addressees to be related to law.[145]

145 On legal symbols in general, see Resnik/Curtis (2011); Goodrich (2013); on images of law and justice Schild (1995); Kocher (1992).

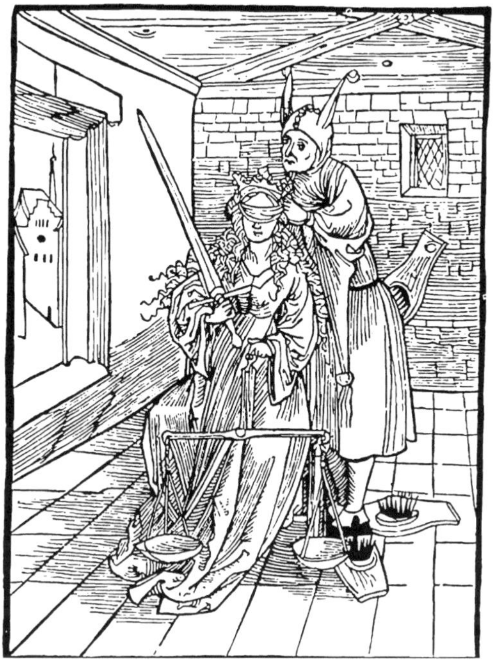

FIGURE 10
Sebastian Brant, The fool blindfolds the eyes of justice, in: Das Narrenschiff (1494)

Among the numerous emblems and symbols of law, the most famous symbol is undoubtedly that of Lady Justice (Justitia), the allegorical personification of the moral force of law (e.g. Fig. 10). As discussed at length in literature, the interpretation of her attributes raises a number of questions, especially since these attributes have not always been uniform and at times even been contradictory.[146] To begin with, historically Lady Justice did not wear a blindfold on every depiction, although today the blindfold is mostly be regarded as her most prominent feature, symbolizing a jurisprudence that is without regard to the persons at bar. But the blindfold can also be understood to mean that the courts are blind to the real facts of life. Moreover, the sword is unquestionably the symbol of physical power, but it is also the sword of the executioner. The scales, on the one hand, may mean the weighing of the soul of the accused and thus of his guilt according to objective criteria of gravity. On the other hand, a more profane reading sees the origins of this instrument in the scales with which the coins were weighed that were due as tax. Moreover, there is the question of gender, which has recently come to the forefront of cultural research. If Lady Justice is a woman, then one might ask, whether this

146 Out of the comprehensive literature on Lady Justice, the personification of justice, see only Jay (1999); Schuster (2005); González García (2017).

is so because the law is weak, and this weakness must be compensated by the sword? Or is Lady Justice a woman because women were supposedly kind and mild? If the formulation of the question in this way proves anything, then that any answers can only be found if one considers the use of gender-specific attributes at the time in which the symbol was devised or when it was being used. A possible answer here might be that Lady Justice which is dressed in her flowing robes was designed as the counter-image to the undressed Phryne,[147] so that "what is threatening in the multitude, i.e. the images as well as women, is banished in the image of the woman embodying justice".[148]

In modern times, symbols were mostly taken from a religious context known to the addressees and reinterpreted according to current needs. One of the best-known examples of such a re-interpretative use is the image of the Leviathan by Abraham Bosse, which adorns the frontispiece of Hobbes' famous state theoretical treatise of the same name from 1651 (Fig. 11), originally a water beast from the book Job.[149] The power of this animal is already "concretized in terms of politics" in the Bible, and it is only by way of Hobbes' re-interpretation that it becomes the symbol of the all-powerful and superior state and as such "probably the most famous metaphor of politics".[150] However, the frontispiece does not seem to completely trust the intended reading of the visual symbol, since the symbol is supplemented by the concluding sentence of the description of the biblical beast with the words: "Non est Potestas super Terram quae comparetur ei" ("There is no power on earth which can be compared to him").[151]

The "eye of the law" is another symbol which was also often used, and which can still be found today, as the traditional Masonic symbol, on the US dollar bill. In its origin, the symbol reaches even further back to the pharaonic times of Egypt.[152] As regards its symbolic meaning, the "eye of the law" prolongs the tradition of the omniscient and the all-seeing eye of God, thus revealing its own as well as law's religious origin. At the same time, the symbol detaches itself from its religious origins to the extent to which law detaches itself from its ritual roots and becomes increasingly secularized over time.[153] In the last

147 For the story of Phryne, the woman accused of indecency and of advocating a false god who proves her innocence by disrobing her clothes in front of the male only jury, see below in the subpart on visual representations of legal actions.

148 Vismann (2007), p. 24.

149 Job 40, 25–41.

150 Bredekamp (2016), p. 11 (translation of the original German quotation by the author).

151 Job 41, 25.

152 Stolleis (2004/2009), pp. 15 et seq.

153 For a contemporary example, see, e.g., www.visual-history.de/2016/10/02/video-oder-was-haben-die-berliner-verkehrsbetriebe-bvg-mit-homer-zu-tun.

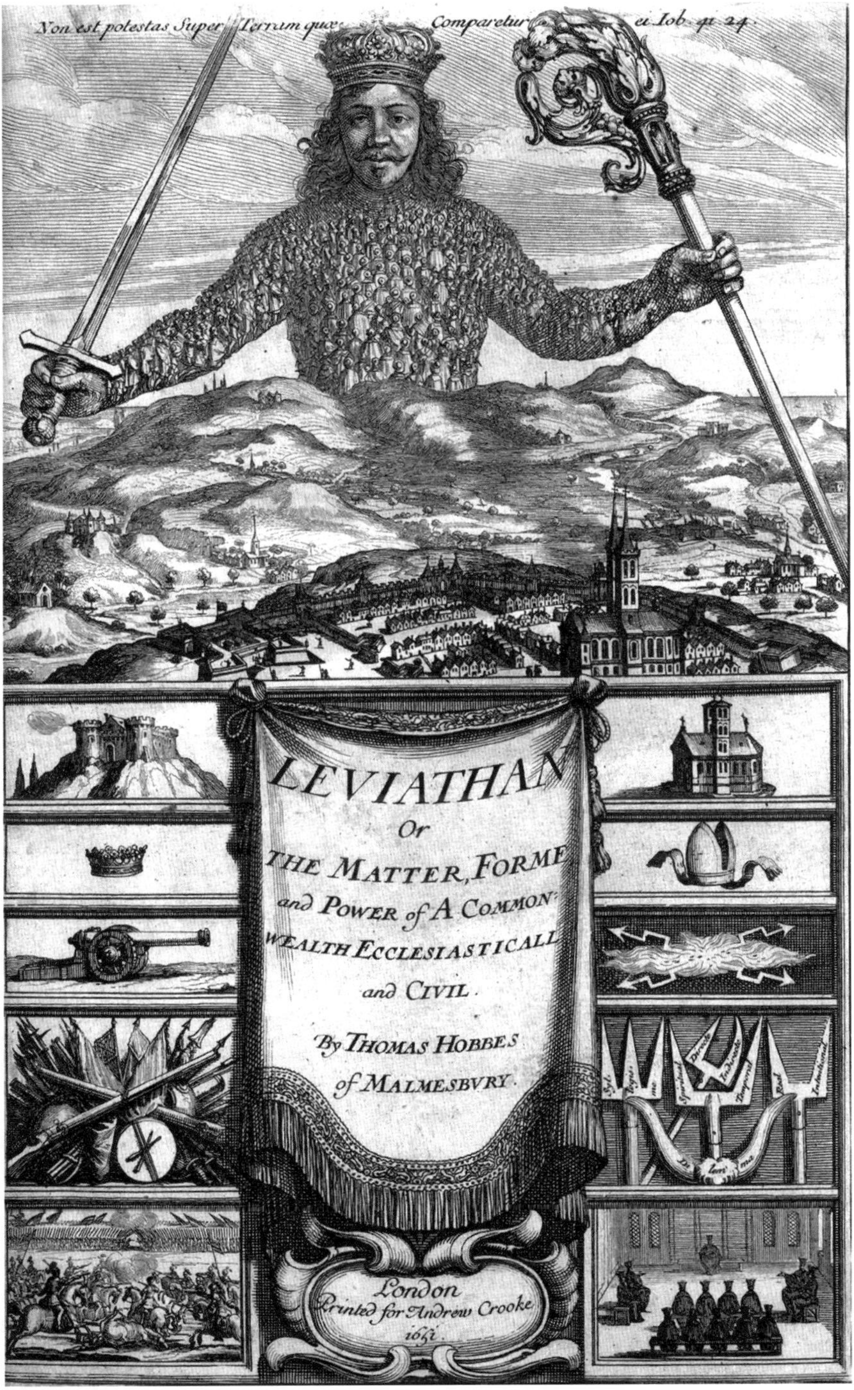

FIGURE 11 Abraham Bosse, Leviathan, Frontispiece of Thomas Hobbes, Leviathan (1651)

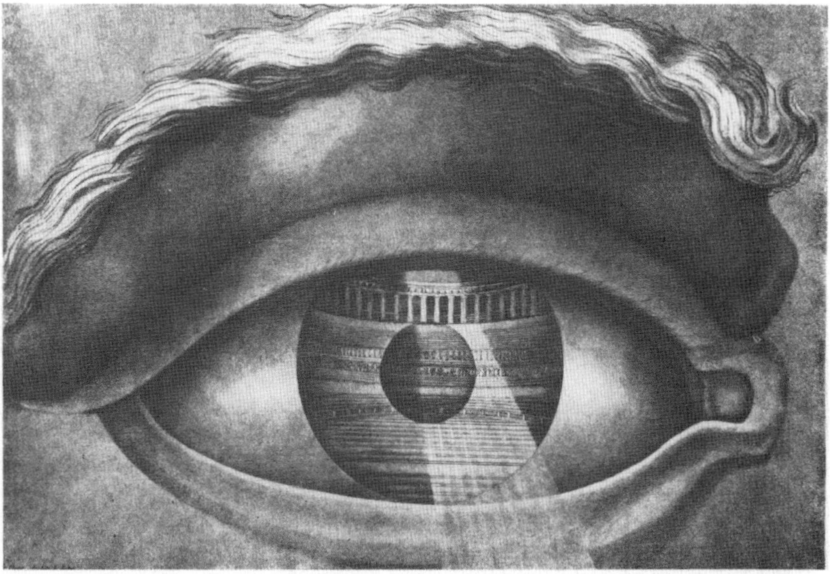

FIGURE 12 Claude Nicolas Ledoux, Interior of the theater of Besancon (1804)

consequence the "eye of the law" no longer stands for the religiously founded power of law, but for its all-encompassing claim to validity, which in its totality is not inferior to the totalitarian conduct of Leviathan. It then hardly comes as a surprise that with the French Revolution the symbol of the eye experiences yet another turn of its state theoretical interpretation (Fig. 12). Here, in connection with the republican programmatic slogan "liberté, fraternité, égalité" ("freedom, fraternity, equality") the eye symbolizes the fundamental state theoretical claim to equality of all citizens. The pictorial representation mostly used for the "eye of the law" clearly ties in with the tradition of the symbolism of the all-seeing eye. However, it is neither a symbol of statutory law nor of the law as an institution. Moreover, it should be noted that the visual representation of the eye often used as a symbol for the law[154] was initially designed, as part of French revolutionary architecture, for the interior of the theatre in Besançon in which according to the republican ideology of equality every spectator should have an equal view of the events on stage.

154 See, e.g., the cover of the book of Stolleis (2004); however, the English translation of the book contains a different depiction of the Eye of God.

5.2.4 Current Symbolism of Law

Undoubtedly, the legibility of such complex symbols with several layers of meaning has declined in recent decades with the dwindling of their social significance and the knowledge of texts and symbols of the classical educational canon.[155] This applies even more to the emblems, which are deliberately far more complex in their levels of meaning. Nevertheless, several symbols still persist today, above all the ambivalent character of the all-seeing eye, which promises both to protect with permanent surveillance and to control and discipline at the same time. This ambiguity lives on, for example, in the official pictogram that is to be affixed, e.g. in Germany, wherever the surrounding space is monitored by an automated video camera (Fig. 13).

Of course, the contemporary stylized video camera as a graphic symbol has been kept much simpler – and, by the way, in a form already outdated – than its precursor of the seeing eye. In contrast to the latter, whose normative power lies precisely in the symbol itself, today's stylized video camera, rather than having any normative force, is merely an informative indicator and a warning signal. At the same time, the replacement of the human eye by a technical apparatus refers to the paradigm shift that has delegated human vision to a mere technical dispositive thus delegating the act of viewing by a human, to the inanimate and hence blind automated machine which in turn becomes the trans-human surveillance authority. At the same time, the pictogram of the surveillance camera refers to the paradigm shift that the concept of "seeing" has undergone over course of this technical and following social development.

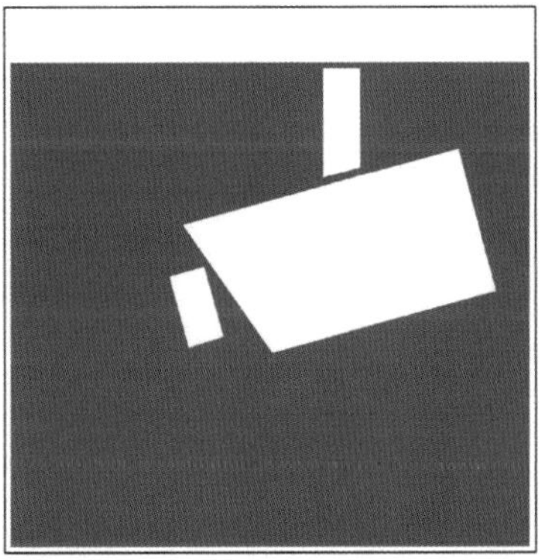

FIGURE 13
Pictogram indicating video surveillance (DIN 33450)

155 Regretting the loss of the classical humanistic educational canon, e.g., Fuhrmann (2002).

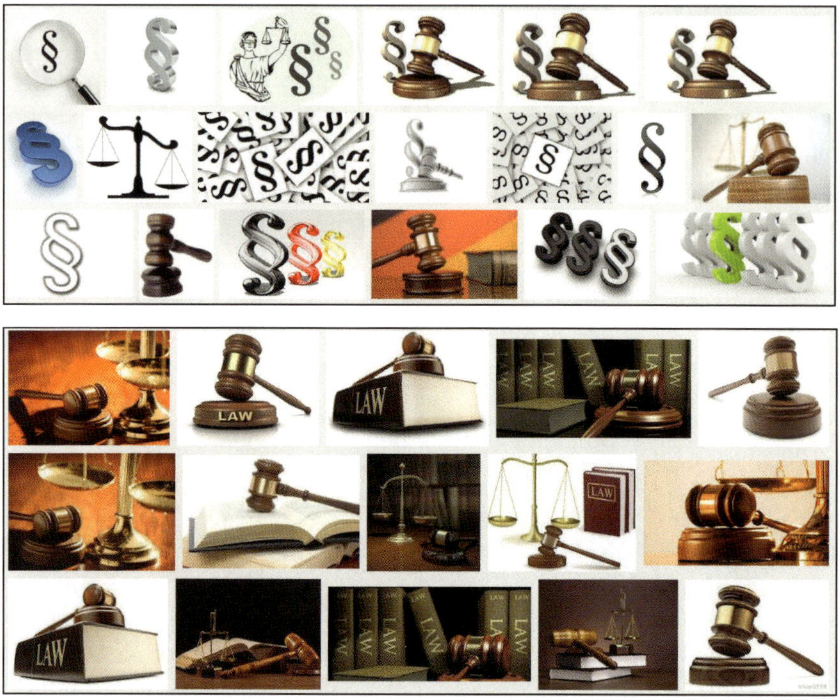

FIGURE 14 Search results for "Recht + Bild" (Google, DE) above and "Law + Image" (Google, UK) below

Furthermore, the simplification of legal symbols leads to the symbol's standardisation and reduction of its complexity. This standardization may lead to quite different results in different legal systems. Indeed, using Google's national image search engines in Germany and the United Kingdom to perform an automated image search on the Internet entering the search words "Recht + Bild" (in Germany) and "Law + Image" (in the United Kingdom), does result in images which substantially differ from each other, as can be seen in Fig. 14.

If one assumes that the ranking of the respective search engines reflects both the frequency of the respective use and the understanding of the searchers of these symbols, the search results indeed correspond to the respective national symbolic culture, which in turn is based on the structure and culture of the respective legal system. In other words, the search results illustrate the different ways in which law and legal actions are staged in the two countries, particularly in court proceedings, and the different ways in which these acts with legal significance are visible to those subject to them. The paragraph symbol ("§") which shows up prominently amongst the German, but not amongst the English search results is a perfect example. Since it is only used in German legal texts both as a written and a visual sign in order to mark and distinguish the norms of a statutory legal text from one another, this sign can only be used and understood as a symbol for the law in Germany, where it works quite effectively because it signals the otherness of, and hence the difference between legal and non-legal texts. In jurisdictions belonging to, or following the tradition of the Anglo-American legal system, the designation of individual legal norms rather is "articles" (in Great Britain) or "sections" (in the USA). It goes without saying that both "articles" ad "sections" cannot fulfil the task of a symbol, since besides appearing in legal texts, these denominations are likewise part of everyday language with a variety of meanings attached to them.

Whereas in Germany, in addition to the "§"-sign some scales and even a few Lady Justices appear amongst the search results, in Great Britain the hammer of the court clearly dominates. It may be somewhat surprising that the hammer also appears among the German search results, although it is not even used in German courts. However, the most probable explanation is that this phenomenon is the result of the rather influential presence of British and above all US-American television series and films that deal with court procedures. However, it is of greater interest regarding the symbolic value of the hammer that this instrument used in the UK courtrooms seems to have less symbolic power in the UK than the paragraph sign in Germany, as may be concluded from the discovery that a hammer hardly ever represents the law alone but is mostly supplemented by the juxtaposition of the image of one or several books. Of course, the reference to the latter directly refers to the text quality of the law. But moreover, since books as such have a rather unspecific character, the word "law" must be applied to the backs of most of the books shown in the symbols found and which accompany the judicial hammer, thus symbolizing the law only together with it. In addition, the visual symbol of the book and thus the symbolic connection between the hammer and the book on the back of which the term "law" is inscribed refers to the legal text while at the same time symbolizing the text of the law in a written way. At the same time, the visual symbol explicitly names the symbolized object of law as what it is. Thus, it is no longer a symbol of law, but the direct designation of the designated object itself.

5.2.5 Schematic Representations in Law

Apart from these examples, images of law are most likely to be used in legal practice mostly in the form of schematic representations of legal contexts.

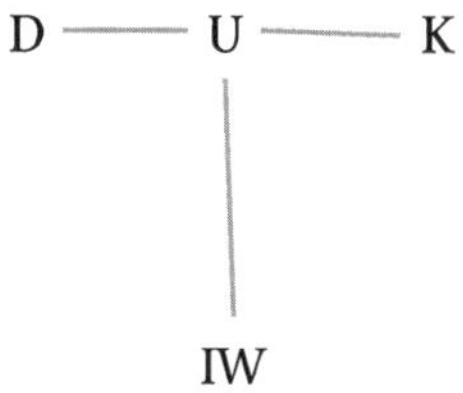

FIGURE 15
Example of a schematic representation of persons involved in a legal case

Every law student learns to keep track of the facts of legal cases in which more than two people are involved with the help of a schematic drawing. Such visual representations, in which the colourful and complex reality has been stripped of all accidental details until the relational structure essential for the decision has been uncovered, tend to be extremely abstract due to the deductive nature of the legal reasoning to be found in countries with a Roman legal tradition. One such example shown in Fig. 15 is based on a case in which an entrepreneur (U for "*Unternehmer*") entrusts a designer (D) with the creation of a website which, on the one hand, is taken over almost identically by a competitor (K for "*Konkurrent*") and, on the other hand, a student of information economics (IW for "*Informationswirtschaft*") who sells it as a screenshot in the form of posters to his fellow students.

Today's students, however, appear to find this type of representation all too Spartan and tend to enrich the representation of the same case constellation with pictures. Apparently, the author of the schematic case representation shown in Fig. 16 held the opinion that pictures have a greater explanatory value if the different persons involved are not merely referred to by individual letters, but by way of images, even if such visual signs are re-usable clip art images. At the same time, just because such clip-art icons can assume different meanings depending on the context in which they are being used, the student author of this schematic case representation obviously felt that the deficits of the visual representation by way of clip-art should, after all, be made up by indications of the relationships amongst the individual participants once again by way of a verbal description. In other words, images of the law are considered necessary here to make the representation more vivid. At the same time, however, the images no longer possess the power that made a semantic informational addition in the form of text superfluous.

This one example could indeed be symptomatic of the current relationship between image and law and at the same time explain why attempts to complement traditional, logocentric jurisprudential doctrine with visual elements ultimately are limited to PowerPoint slides, video recordings of lectures and photographs by professors and lecturers.[156] This is notwithstanding the fact

156 On legal visualisation in general, see Röhl/Ulbrich (2007); Hilgendorf (2005).

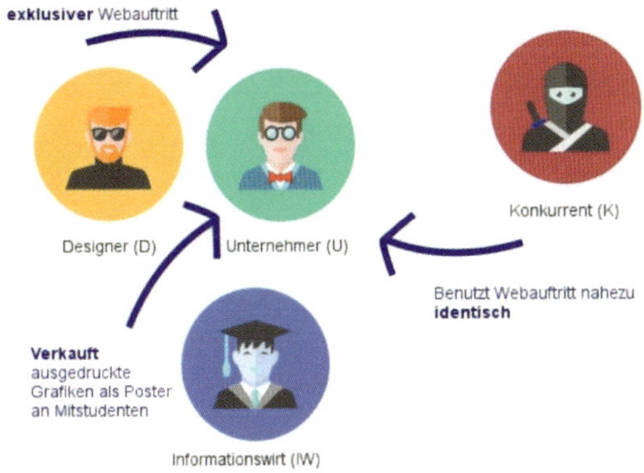

FIGURE 16 Nadim Hammoud, Schematic representation of the same case as in Fig. 15

that the affinity of the younger generation for images is undoubtedly greater than the one of older law professors and practitioners with their strong belief that the authoritative power of text-bound law be best preserved by the law's traditional image phobia, which still makes them view the use of images even in PowerPoint presentations with great scepticism. Likewise, another factor prevents the images from increasingly invading the so far foreign territory of the law. True, the cost of image recording devices may be becoming cheaper, and the recording devices may become easier to use. But it still requires a considerable amount of time and skills to produce moving images of law and legal actions which aesthetically may compete with professional formats of television and, above all, film narratives which attract and retain the viewers' attention. The production of truly illuminating legal images requires not only substantial legal but also a visual competency, which lawyers usually do not possess. The ultimately failed attempts to visually enrich legal doctrine through popular pictorial forms such as, above all, comic drawings have demonstrated that in these cases too much and too fuzzy information is carried into the legal text, which is not neither necessary for a better understanding of conflict-laden disputes, nor helpful for their legal solution.

Hence, for the time being images in law are mainly limited to schematizing illustrations of the sort of the graphic overview of legal areas of law, such as the famous example concerning the different branches of intellectual property legislation, borrowed from the pages of Wikipedia (Fig. 17).

An external influence for an increase in the visualization of law and legal matters could, however, emanate from the attempt to structure legal statutes and legal argumentations to be automatically produced, interpreted and

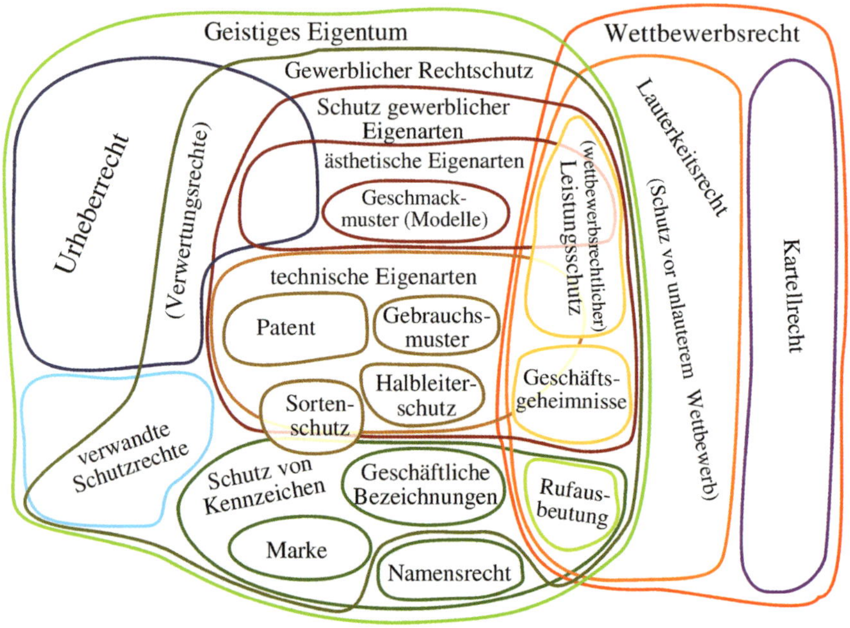

FIGURE 17 Visualization of the legal areas of intellectual property law at Wikipedia

applied by automated IT-systems. The formalization of law required in designing such systems will evidently lead to visual representations of the relationships amongst legal norms and their individual components in the form of a model[157] that may be regarded as an "image" in much the same way, as the legal norm can be described as a visualized model of reality.[158]

5.2.6 Visual Representations of Legal Actions

Unquestionably, the most traditional example of the depiction of judicial "law in action" in painting is the subject of the Last Judgement. Stefan Lochner's version from the year 1435 shown here shall only serve as an illustrative example (Fig. 18).[159] This subject refers to the central content of faith and the last earthly instance of an eschatologically oriented Christian theology. What is depicted is the retrospective assessment of the moral life of those standing in court and thus a moral reflection of human life in general. Jurisprudence is an

157 See, e.g., Kreuzbauer (2005); Raabe/Oberle/Baumann/Wacker/Funk (2012).

158 For a more detailed discussion of the model aspect of legal norms see below, part 4.2.

159 See only the overview in Christe (2001); and for a cross-section of legal visualisation from an art-historical point of view Kern (2005).

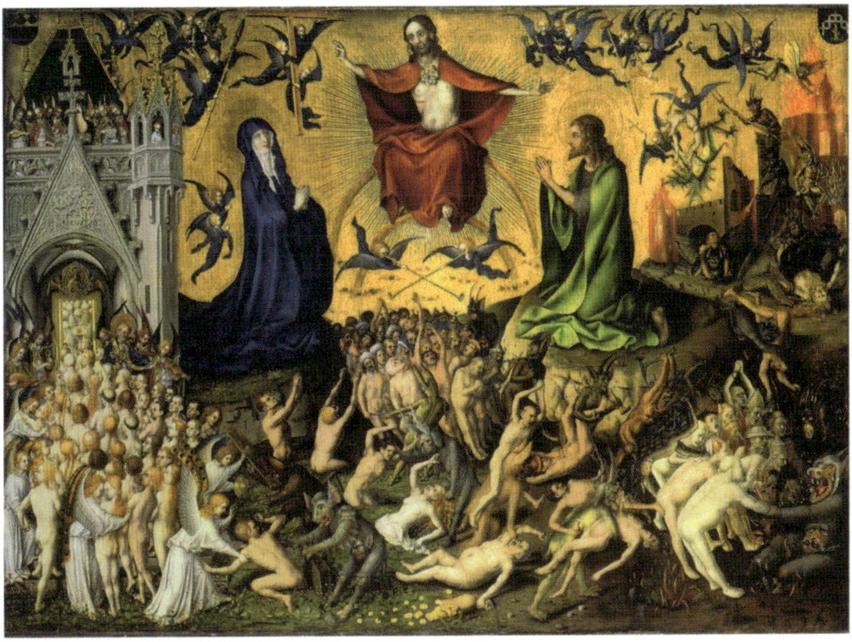

FIGURE 18 Stefan Lochner, The Last Judgement (1435)

activity of evaluation and of judgment, which leads to a conclusion of granting salvation or pronouncing damnation. As a background for the depiction of the fear of existence and hope for the heavenly afterlife of the believers suffering from earthly fate, depictions of the Last Judgement are always powerful in their presentation of the torments of hell and, at the same time, in their vivid depictions of moral reproaches and threats. What is called for is the religious obedience of those who look at such pictures. Therefore, paintings of the Last Judgement have generally been given a prominent place in the architecturally coordinated picture programmes of churches. Quite like the later symbols and images of a secularized law, the representations of the Last Judgement embody the claim of an omnipresent and universal power and of the rule of the Almighty God as ultimate judge, against whose final judgment no appeal is possible.

It was only after the iron grip of the totalitarian claim of religion increasingly loosened a few centuries later that other representations of judicial practice become possible. Mostly, symbolic stories of ancient texts served as the point of reference for the symbolic representation of practical legal events, such as the episode depicted by Jean-Léon Gérôme in 1861 (Fig. 19). As this story has it, the Greek courtesan (*hetaera*, ἑταίρα) who had discarded her clothes

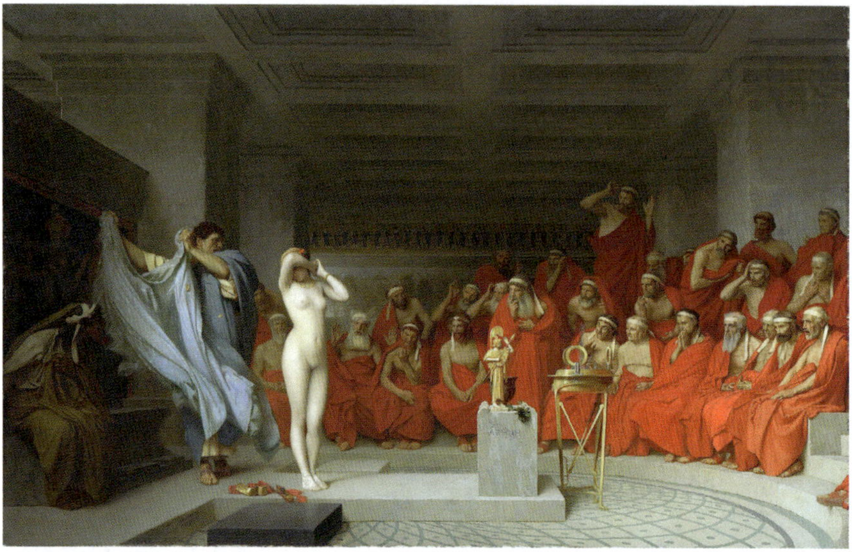

FIGURE 19 Jean-Léon Gérôme, Phryne before the Areopagus (ca. 1861)

before the Areopagus, was acquitted of the accusation of shamelessness and of propagating of a new deity.[160] It goes without saying that this depiction transforms a textual episode into a visual representation, thus satisfying the sensual pleasure of the picture's male observers, since quite clearly the female nudity in the picture in front of a male only jury of elderly judges is not motivated solely by the events depicted, but is also staged with the (male) observer in mind who can easily identify himself with, and blend into the crowd of elderly male onlookers. But it is likewise possible to demonstrate the primacy of pictorial beauty over the medium of speech used for the defence and in the text of the law, according to which the acquittal should presumably not have taken place. Of course, if one would have wanted to fully grasp the meaning of the painting and the relationship between image and text, one would most of all have had to be familiar with the written text that handed down the episode.

This already comparatively late depiction of an ancient mythological court scene, which is only cited here as an example, is at the same time part of the series of paintings that discuss the borderline, marked by the clothing,

160 McClure (2003), pp. 41 et seq.; in symbolic terms, it is irrelevant that the undressing may not have taken place in this way, see Cooper (1995); on the imagery of justice (Dike) in competition with beauty (Aphrodite) and the integration of images into the proper order of law see Vismann (2007), p. 22 et seq.

between the private self and the surrounding public space with regard to its public displayability which once again is defined by normative rules.[161] Only two years later, Manet's "Olympia", by severing the tie to any mythological source, elevates this issue to the very theme of the painting, deliberately contradicting the aesthetic norm of Manet's time, which required a semantic clothing of nudity. The provocation inherent in the not only physical, but at the same time no longer mythically or allegorically motivated disrobing of the prostitute depicted in Manet's painting inevitably scandalized the salon audience of the time.

At the end of the historical detachment of law and legal actions from their religious roots and mythological references stands the completely profaned everyday life in court, degenerated to ridicule by the egoisms of its small-minded participants and perverted to greed and ultimately to petty bourgeois miserliness as targeted by Honoré Daumier in his numerous caricatures full of criticism and biting mockery, which stands in strong opposition to the original idea of justice rooted in the divine (Fig. 20).

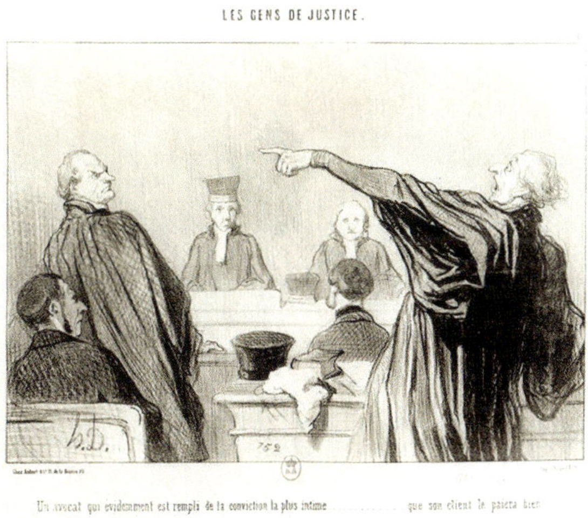

FIGURE 20 Honoré Daumier, Les gens de justice: "Un avocat qui evidemment est rempli de la conviction la plus intime … que son client le paiera bien" (ca. 1845). Note: "A lawyer who is obviously filled with the most intimate conviction … that his client will pay him well."

161 See, e.g., Köhler (2013).

Finally, this brief overview of images of law and legal actions would remain incomplete if one were not to mention the representation of judicial practice in the form of court proceedings shown especially in American film classics. These movies range from "Witness for the Prosecution" with Charles Laughton's embodiment of the judge, and "12 Angry Men" by director Sidney Lumet to the cinematographic re-enactment of the Nuremberg Trials under the title "Judgement at Nuremberg" with Maximilian Schell in the role of the defender who asserts the defence of supra-statutory emergency for the accused Nazi criminals. These films have shaped the idea of legal proceedings of a whole generation as much as todays' innumerable courtroom series and entertainment formats of staged courtroom TV-shows. If such formats almost exclusively concern criminal proceedings and, in addition, only reflect Anglo-American judicial practices, this is to be explained by the rather abstract way in which civil law procedures are conducted in countries which stand in the tradition of Roman law. In addition, unlike the US, where the criminal proceedings against the football player O.J. Simpson degenerated into a true media spectacle, countries with a more longstanding legal tradition show a much greater reserve towards the creation of a media public, even if judicial proceedings as such are generally open to the public. But that public is one only of the courtroom.[162]

5.2.7 Staged Representations of the Law

Finally, the representation of law by itself, i.e. the structure of court proceedings as tribunals, the courtroom as stage and/or theatre can only briefly be mentioned and shall not be discussed in detail, since the focus here is on images of law.[163] However, mention shall be made of the visual representation of law by way of observation, depiction and documentation of legal acts

162 In Germany, the restraint towards public transmissions and visual recordings of court proceedings was not fundamentally changed by the recent reform by the Act on the Expansion of the Media Public in Court Proceedings (Gesetz über die Erweiterung der Medienöffentlichkeit in Gerichtsverfahren, EMöGG) of October 2017. According to this new legislation, only announcements of decisions may be filmed and televised, as was already permitted before as far as judgements of the Federal Constitutional Court were concerned. However, the court proceedings as such continue to remain closed to observation by the media; see Official Journal (BGBl.) 2017 I p. 3546; on this issue see Schübel (2017); critical Brodocz (2007); for possibilities and limits of litigation PR see Boehme-Neßler (2010).

163 From the wealth of literature on these issues see only the contributions in Gephart/Leko (2017); and, in particular, on the legal symbolism in courtrooms and court buildings as exemplified by the interim building of the German Constitutional Court Dreier (2019), pp. 133 et seq.

not – as in the case of the above-mentioned court series and court shows – for the purpose of entertainment, but for a normative representation of the law. A prominent example of this sub-category of images of law can be seen in the visual documentation of the signing of Germany's Basic Law in the year 1949. Rather than being just an external documentation of the signing procedure, the photographs undertake to support and accentuate the normative significance of the event, thus themselves transporting a normative appeal. The art historian Horst Bredekamp has painstakingly analysed to what extent the ostensibly documentary depiction of this act, which was so important for the Federal Republic of Germany in terms of legal policy, is characterized by the aesthetics of the provisional, almost accidental. What was developed in harmony with the thrifty symbols of the young republic which were consciously designed in contrast to the brutish visual language used by National Socialism and without any pompous self-representation was a visual language which constituted a very peculiar and independent symbol of modesty.[164]

In a broader sense, images of law can ultimately be understood as including visual representations that neither symbolise law nor depict any of its components or its application, but rather, by means of artistic reflection, thematise the institution of law as such or at least some of its aspects. In view of the still far-reaching separation of the legal from the artistic sphere, such artistic works dedicated to law are not very numerous. Theoretically, however, a comparatively broad spectrum opens up here, as can be demonstrated by the examples taken from Karlsruhe, the German city which is the location of both Germany's Constitutional and Federal Supreme Court and which is therefore nicknamed "residence of law" ("*Residenz des Rechts*"). In Karlsruhe, an installation designed by Jochen Gerz and entitled "Place of Fundamental Rights" located in front of the city castle, does not make use of the text of fundamental rights as formulated in Germany's Basic Law. Rather, the individual panels mounted on flagpoles which in their entirety are distributed over the place as well as across the city each show a short citation taken from a statement concerning the law, legal rules and the legal order made by a select number of city representatives and of the public at large (Fig. 21).[165]

164 Bredekamp (2011).

165 Gerz (2006). – For a citation of the interview by the artist of the author, see ibid., pp. 31 and 103 ("Es kann nicht sein, dass wir uns Regeln ausdenken, die zwar vorhersehbar sind, aber vielen Menschen gegen den Strich gehen. Auf der einen Seite müssen wir mit der Komplexität der Welt fertig werden, zum anderen können wir im Einzelfall in unserer täglichen Umgebung nur mit Rechtsregeln umgehen, die eine bestimmte Simplizität haben"; "It is not acceptable that we make up rules that are predictable, but that go against the grain for many people. On the one hand, we have to cope with the complexity

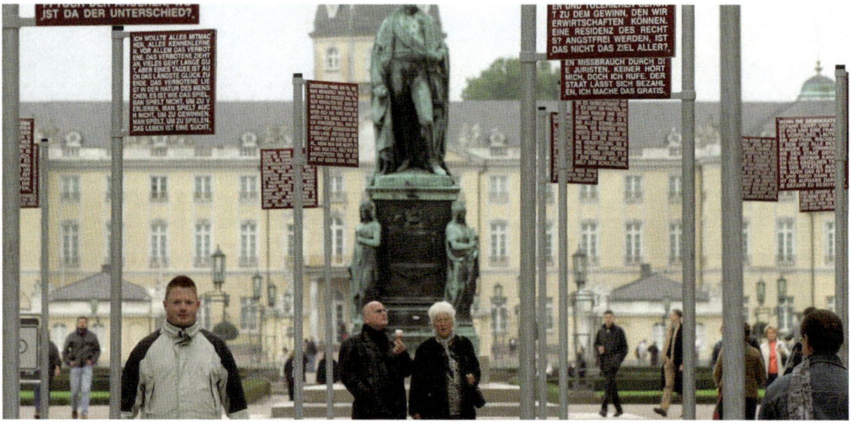

FIGURE 21 Jochen Gerz, Place of Fundamental Rights, Karlsruhe (2005)

Further examples were on display attached to the fence which surrounded the Federal Constitutional Court during its renovation in 2012.[166] In one of the three artistic installations, situations relevant to fundamental rights were discussed in critical refraction by way of photographs of the holders of the respective fundamental rights (Fig. 22). Another installation focused on the transparency of the building which houses the German Constitutional Court,[167] and a third installation examined, and made visible, the internal structure of the language used in constitutional decisions handed down by the German Constitutional Court by way of arranging the words of several key decisions – including all the punctuation marks – in strictly alphabetical order. The resulting pattern made visible which role prohibitions ("not"; "forbidden", etc.) play in the decisions, and what significance differentiating exceptions have, which in German court rulings are generally marked by the word "fundamentally" ("*grundsätzlich*"), which contrary to its meaning in everyday language does not state how things are usually dealt with, but rather refers to the exception to the principle set out in the respective sentence which affects the specific case to be decided (Fig. 23).

of the world; on the other hand, in individual cases we can only deal with rules of law in our daily environment, which are of a certain simplicity").

166 Albus (2014); a video documentation of the three artistic installations can be found at https://vimeo.com/36288672 and http://www.schlossbezirk3.de.

167 Gompf, V.S./Miletzki, J: Perspektivenwechsel (2012); on this subject see also Jaeger (2014); Dreier (2017) and (2019).

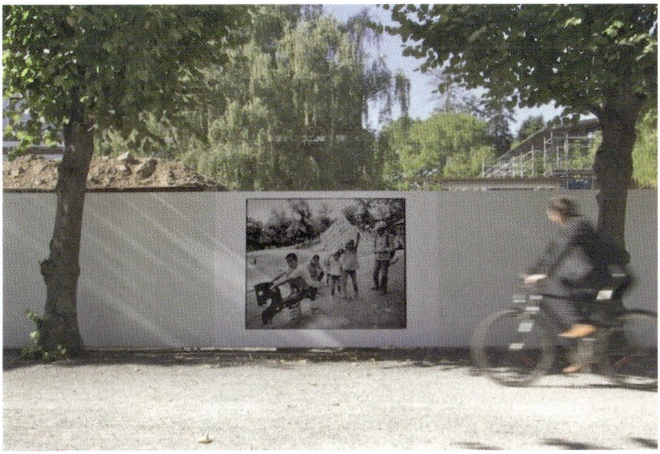

FIGURE 22 Milz/Erbe/Jähde, Civil Rights (2012)

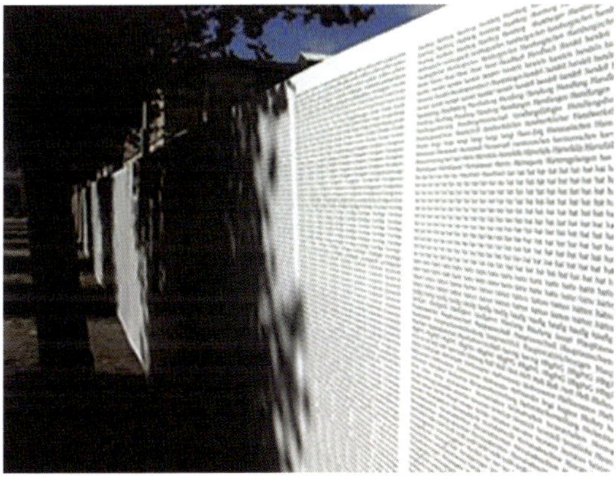

FIGURE 23
Stach, Judgements of the Constitutional Court – Remix (2012)

5.3 *Images for Law*

In addition to the images *in* law and those *of* law that are usually mentioned when the subject of law and images is addressed, the third category of images *for* law has so far hardly ever been addressed and systematically thematised. These images which serve the operation of law and hence the functioning of the legal system in general, can be divided in two categories. The classical category is the one of mostly photographs, but also of visualisations of text which are used in legal procedures as images of evidence. However, with digitisation a second category has formed which consists of images that are created by a machine in order to be processed by the same or another machine in the process of automatically applying legal rules.

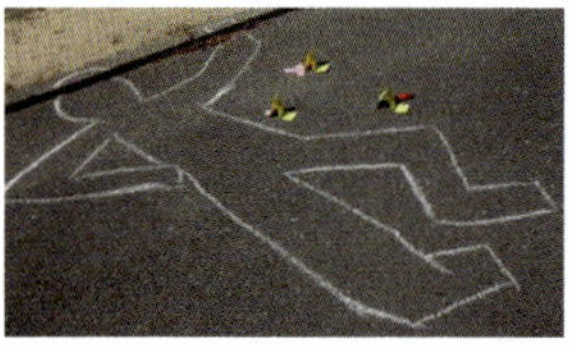

FIGURE 24
Example of a photograph taken for documenting evidence later to be used in legal proceedings
PHOTO: GESINE KUHLMANN

To begin with the first of these two categories, traditionally, images of evidence which serve the operation of law and hence the functioning of the legal system, are taken for *repressive* purposes. Such images are taken to document certain details of crimes that have already been committed to enable law enforcement (Fig. 24). However, in the beginning, the use of photographs as evidence in legal court proceedings was all but undisputed. As already mentioned above,[168] the question at issue was to whom, to the narrated story or to the sensory image, greater trust should be placed in ascertaining the facts in a legal proceeding. The doubts that were raised in this respect resulted from the fact that contrary to the testimony of eye witnesses, photographic evidence of the place or the tools used in committing a crime were initially considered as merely indirect evidence. Although by now, photographic evidence is as such permitted as evidence in most countries simply because it generally considered as being more precise than the generally flawed memory of eyewitnesses. However, doubts persist – and hence must be overcome – regarding the continuity of the indexical trace which links the depiction of an object that can be seen in a certain photograph which is introduced into legal court proceedings to the object depicted by the photograph. Of course, the belief in the objectivity of photographs was stronger in the field of analogue photography than is now regarding results of digital photography. The reason simply is that analogue photography was more difficult to manipulate than digital photography. Since the Public Prosecutor's Office which bases its indictment on photographs as evidence, must show that the photographs it submits as evidence have not been tampered with, there is a need for technical safeguards to ensure that there has been no unauthorised interference between the taking and use of the photograph introduced as evidence in the trial. And if today, the courts are still reluctant to admit recordings of dashcams as evidence of traffic offences, this reluctance is not so much rooted in doubts as to the accuracy or directness of the recordings, but rather in the effort to protect the personality rights of the other road users who did not commit the incriminated traffic offense.[169]

168 For references and discussion see above 2.3.

169 For German law see BGH of 15 May 2018, VI ZR 233/17, NJW 2018, pp. 883 et seq.

Moreover, due to the increasing focus on aspects of security, photographs of evidence taken for the purposes of repressive criminal prosecution are increasingly accompanied by photographs taken for *preventive* purposes. These images are intended to ensure, by way of omnivoyance, that ideally no criminal offences will be committed in the first place.[170] Of course, such images are not entirely novel. Already in the 19th century, criminalistics and jurisprudence were taking – in a method called phrenology – the physiological shape of the skull (craniology) as well as of the shape of the face and the brain. Such images were taken as the starting point for the assumption of a relationship between these visual forms and the character, with the aim of making a prognosis regarding the propensity of the person in question to commit future criminal acts.[171] Today, for legal purposes such recordings are mainly produced by surveillance cameras which are increasingly installed in public as well as in private places. However, contrary to what is claimed by the narrative developed to justify their installation, surveillance cameras have so far not been able to prevent crimes. Even the expansion of the areas monitored, an improvement in the quality of the images taken, as well as faster automated image evaluation by self-learning computer programs, which tend to replace the error-prone human observer will not be able to prevent the emergence of crimes. At best, they lead to a relocation of criminal activities to unmonitored areas, provided, of course, that such unmonitored areas will still exist in the future.[172] It follows that such surveillance arrangements are ultimately merely repressive in nature. However, at least images generated by body scanners at airports (Fig. 25)

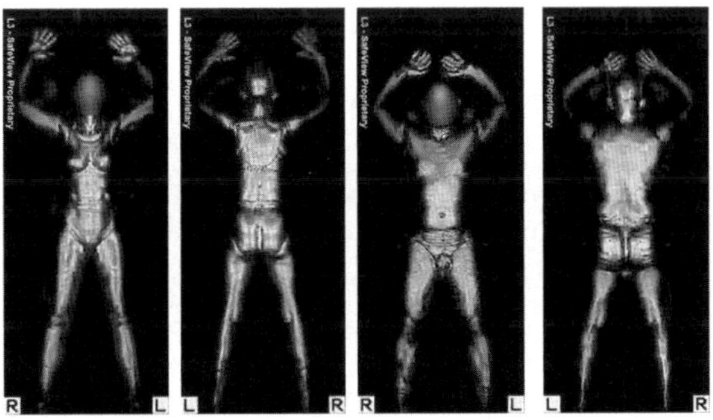

FIGURE 25 Images taken by a body scanner

170 For "omnivoyance", considered as a "Western Europe's totalitarian ambition," see Virilio (1994), p. 33.

171 For the role plaid by photography in the context of surveillance and control in general, see Foucault (1975); Tagg (1988), pp. 66 et seq.; for the progressive intrusion into the body see Siebenpfeiffer (2007); Belting (2017), pp. 63 et seq.

172 See only Kammerer (2008), pp. 345 ff.

may have a preventative effect in that they are produced precisely to prevent, to the extent possible, crimes committed with weapons or explosives in the area beyond the controlling scanner. As of now, it is difficult to foresee to what extent such genuinely preventive devices will be used in the future. However, they are most likely to prevail within the framework of access controls to crime intensive or highly sensitive spatial areas to be protected against attacks, as is already the case today, for example, where such technological protection devices are being used to monitor, control and police access to soccer stadiums.

Little attention, however, has so far been paid to images *for* law which are no longer made to be looked at by a human observer, but which have been intended from the outset to be processed by machines in the course of actions motivated by legal norm, although such images were already foreseen as early as in the late 80s of the last century by the French philosopher Virilio.[173] This categorical substitution of the human eye as the viewing apparatus by an information technology recording and interpretation dispositive makes it appear appropriate to speak of "images for machines". Images for machines can still be categorized as images in that the visual product of the machine possesses all the features of a traditional image, i.e., if a human viewer looks at them, these images for machines do look like images produced by humans, even if only with the help of a machine. Biometric passport photographs, which have been mandatory for official identity documents in the EU (Fig. 26), are a perfect example for such images. These images are highly standardized by normative regulation both as regards their size (45 mm high by 35 mm wide with the depiction of the face from the crown of the head to the chin between 29 mm and 34 mm), iconographic form (a close-up of full head and shoulders; only of the bearer with no other objects or people) and facial expression (facing forward and looking straight at the camera; with a neutral expression and the mouth closed; without anything covering the face; in clear contrast to the background; without a head covering, unless it is worn for religious or medical reasons; with eyes open, visible and free from reflection or glare from glasses; with the eyes not covered by sunglasses, tinted glasses, glasses frames or hair; without any 'red eye', and without any shadows in the picture). In addition, there are a couple of technical requirements to be followed (the photograph must be in colour on plain white photographic paper; taken against a plain cream or light grey background; clear and in focus; taken within the last month; without any creases or tears; unmarked on both sides; unaltered by computer software).[174]

173 Virilio (1994), p. 60.

174 www.gov.uk/photos-for-passports; for discussion see also Dreier (2017).

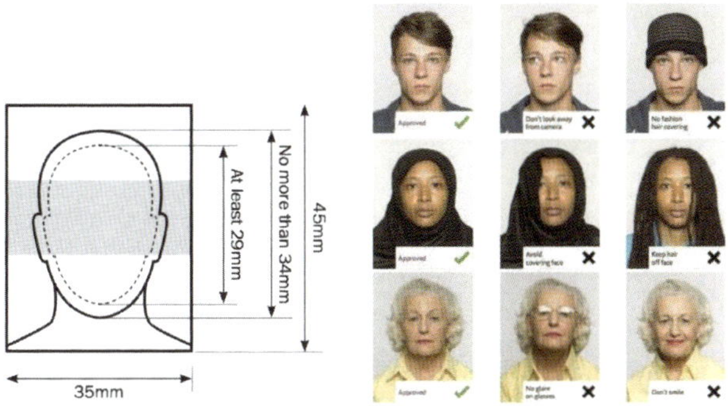

FIGURE 26 Official UK requirements for passport photographs

It is true, the images created in this way still look like photographic images. However, they have little in common with classical portraits, the tradition of which dates back to the Renaissance. Biometric images are no longer about the resemblance between a person and his image, nor about the representation of his character traits, his social status and the traces of his life inscribed on his face. Rather, since the viewer of such pictures is no longer a human being – the border policeman, who compares the picture with the holder of the ID document only carries out a first, fleeting plausibility check – but the computer, i.e. the machine. The issue is one of reading out data from the image and comparing these data with previously recorded data taken either from the same image in other contexts or by other similar images for the purpose of determining when the person concerned crossed a border and at which location, as well as to find out in which context a particular person was registered before and for what reason. Biometric passport photographs are therefore no longer about depicting a human being in the humanistic sense. Rather, their raison d'être is their machine readability and identifiability. In other words, the logic of the surveillance state, into which the biometric passport images are embedded, aims at what might be called informational singularity, i.e. unequivocal identifiability, and no longer at semantic individuality in the sense of representing the personality of the human being depicted. At the same time, the image and normative regulation of biometric passport photographs are intertwined in several ways. As already spelled out, the criteria according to which the images must be produced are normatively specified. In addition, the images are used in the normative context of identification. Above all, the standardization of the image is based on a normatively described model of the face, which also explains why biometric passport photographs are not about similarity in the conventional sense between the photograph and the person photographed. Since quite like a fingerprint, human faces are individually characterized by a

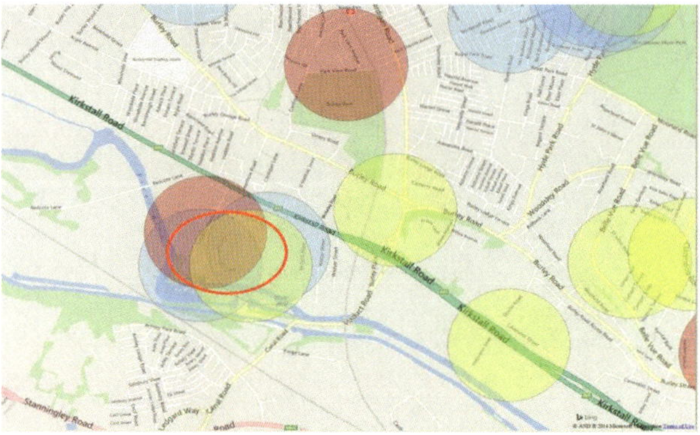

FIGURE 27 "Predictive policing" – visualization of machine-calculated probabilities of crime focal points

comparatively small number of parameters, such as the distance between the eyes, the ratio of the distance between the forehead and the tip of the nose to the distance between the tip of the nose and the chin, etc., the point of reference for both the photograph and its evaluation is ultimately not the complete image visible to the human observer, but the data taken for the purpose of this greatly reduced model of the human face. The definition of this model of the human face constitutes the actual normative core of biometric passport photographs, which is embedded in the image-processing algorithm and, as such, beyond democratic control.[175]

But even beyond facial images, images are created for machines, which then evaluate these images and, for a better understanding of the human being, make them visible in the form of what looks like traditional images. One such example are images created out of data in the context of so-called "predictive policing", i.e. data generated and subsequently visualized when the police bases its controls on predictions about the probability of locations chosen by perpetrators of future crimes, which in turn are derived from the patterns of past crimes (Fig. 27).

As such, the "images" on which the algorithmic probability calculation is based exist only in the form of data and, since they are intended solely for the computer, remain as such invisible. In other words, the visualized identification of the crime focal points merely represents the data that resulted from the computer's calculations. However, such visualisation is needed only if human police officers decide to go on patrol in the designated places.

175 On biometrics as a political agenda, see, e.g., Kurz (2008).

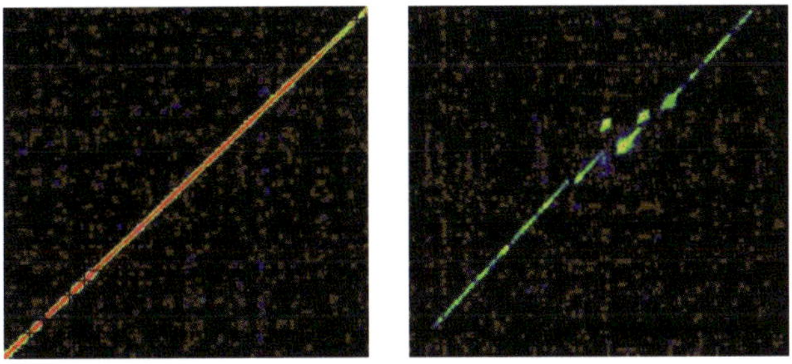

FIGURE 28 Visualisation of exact (left) and near (right) match of video-files uploaded at YouTube.

It follows that this intermediate step of visualizing data so that they can be perceived as images by a human viewer may as well be omitted, if the evaluation and enforcement take place in an automated way by the machine itself. An example of such "images *of* machines as well as *for* machines" are visual representations of the matching results found by upload filters which are used by the platform "YouTube" and which enables users to upload files with potentially copyright infringing material. The filters compare the music and video files uploaded by the users with reference files made available by the holders of the rights to the original works. As appealing as such visualisations might be for the human eye (Fig. 28), for law enforcement these visualisations can ultimately be dispensed with. In contrast to the seeing human eye, the calculating computer is no longer "interested" in images, but only in the data to be processed. As a result, the images for machines disappear behind the data, which increasingly assume their place in the centre of the normative sphere. At the same time, the human is pushed to the edge of the automated event and at best tolerated to the extent that the machine – and thus its constructors, i.e. the authors of the algorithms – gives him the opportunity to look at the images on which the automated decision is based.

In the future, the relationship between image and law will therefore crucially depend on the extent to which the computer scientists who write the programs can be held normatively responsible for the fact that the images which form the basis of the automated calculations be made available for inspection and democratic control.[176]

176 On the approach to shift the emphasis of the control from how the algorithms process data to verifying the correct functioning of the algorithms, see Desai/Kroll (2017).

6 The Normative Effect of Images and the Image Quality of Law

Finally, the question is to be answered whether and, if so, to what extent and under which conditions, images themselves can be said to have a normative quality.[177] In other words, to what extent are images able to have a normative effect or at least to carry a normative appeal? From an opposite direction, it is not only possible to ask about the normativity of images, but likewise about the image quality of legal norms.

6.1 *The Normative Effect of Images*

To begin with, the first of these two questions which asks about the normative appeal inherent in images can easily be answered for traffic signs which represent in and of themselves the respective underlying legal norm in a symbolic way, associated with the threat of enforcement of a legal sanction in the event of non-compliance with the legal command. Likewise, pictograms can be described as instructions for action, even if unlike traffic signs they are not associated with a legal sanction in the event of non-compliance.[178]

Moreover, one might add all those images which carry a moral impetus within them, i.e. which are designed to instruct the viewer about what is right and what is wrong, what is good and what is bad.

This is particularly true for images of the last judgement, in which – apart from showing a legal court procedure – normativity is well reflected by symbols that stand in for actions considered as bad (the "if" of a legal norm) and by depictions of the punishment that awaits the damned (the "then" of a legal norm). The same moral program underlies – albeit usually depicted in a somewhat less drastic manner – most, if not all, religious paintings the purpose of which is to instruct the viewers in the true faith and direct their thinking and behaviour towards the one and only god. Moreover, images which are designed to propagate other, non-religious ideologies, and which directly address the viewers to move them to behave as desired by the rulers and the prevailing ideology can be analysed in a similar way. The Stalinist artistic production is a good example to this effect, although it has to be noted that images in the style of social realism are mostly limited to symbolize the "good" side, leaving the "bad" and its consequences to the darkness of real life torture chambers.

But what about the normative character of images in general? True, images lack the fundamental structure of legal norms. Apart from the traffic signs just mentioned and, in a different way the images of the last judgement, images

177 Gephart/Leko (2017a), pp. 11 et seq.

178 For an overview of pictograms see Christian (2017).

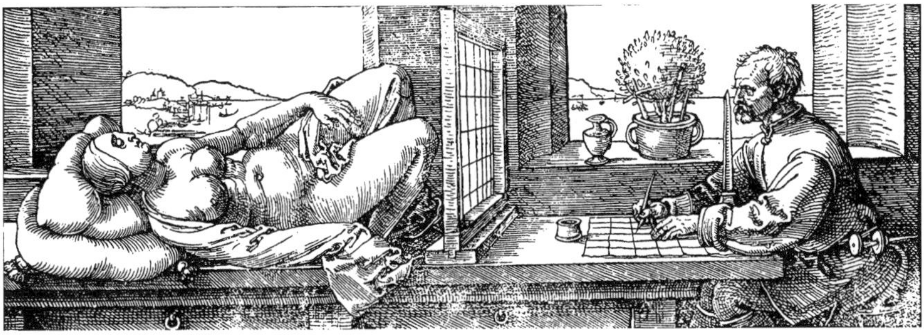

FIGURE 29 Dürer, Draughtsman Drawing a Recumbent Woman, (ca. 1538)

in general do not possess the "if"–"then"-structure which is typical for legal norms, where the "if" defines a certain set of facts which, once they are present, triggers the legal consequence (the "then") indicated in the very same legal norm.

However, independent from the hermeneutic interpretation of their contents, one may well identify a normative quality of images, because images, once they are looked at, incite a certain reaction of the respective viewers. Especially, pictures designed according to the rules of the central perspective as re-discovered from antiquity by Leon Battista Alberti,[179] do in fact exert a certain normative effect on the viewer. As instructively illustrated by Dürer's famous woodcut entitled "Draughtsman Drawing a Recumbent Woman" ("Der Zeichner des liegenden Weibes", Fig. 29), the artist who devises a two-dimensional representation of a pictorial space defines a point inside this space, from which – and only from which – the viewer is able to see what is represented in the picture. No matter from which angle and from which distance the observer looks at a picture, he always looks at it from that very same point of view. The observer is thus placed into the pictorial space and is forced in some sort of self-executing way, to look at the picture from the view point assigned to him by the artist as the normative view point. That is even more true in the case of photography, where the point of view is invariably defined by the place occupied by the camera at the time when the photograph was taken.

An even greater normative force emanating from the perspective in which a picture is construed can, however, be found in the mono-focally construed baroque ceiling paintings, such as Andrea Pozzo's masterly nave ceiling of the Church of Sant'Ignazio in Rome (Fig. 30), where a marking recessed into the church floor indicates the only point within the whole building from which all foreshortened figures in the ceiling can be correctly seen. In his treatise on

179 Alberti, *De pictura* (1435/1436).

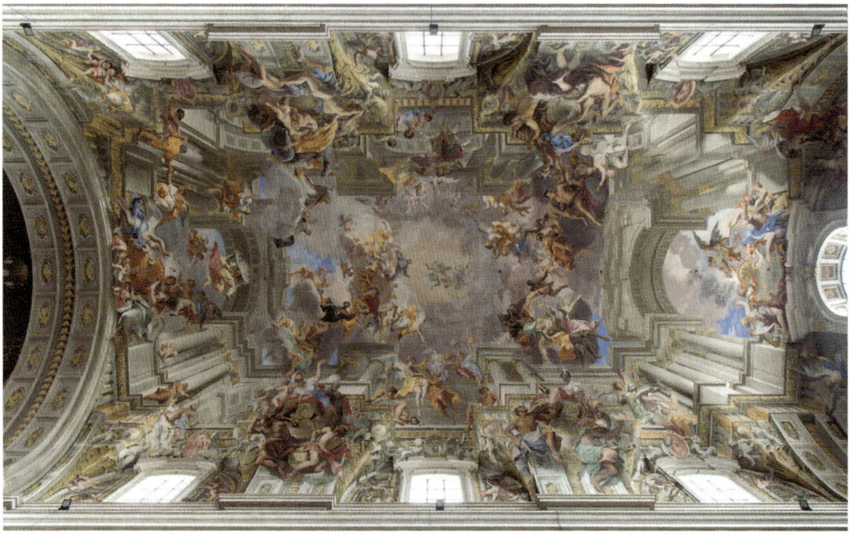

FIGURE 30 Andrea Pozzo, Nave ceiling painting, Sant'Ignazio, Rome (1691–1694)

the perspective of paintings and architecture, Pozzo explicitly describes the normative character of his pictorial constructions by explaining the one focal point as the one true point of viewing god.[180] The act of seeing is normatively guided to enable the viewer to experience the divine presence, and hence linked to the normativity of faith itself. But even in the case of multi-focal ceiling paintings which allow for several points from which different parts of the painting appear correct in perspective, the viewer who wants to see all parts of the painting in the correct mode is guided – albeit in a somewhat less strict and more playful way – to take a pre-defined, and hence normative, course.

But even without the theological connotations just mentioned, images may exercise a normative effect for mainly two reasons.

Firstly, according to classical idealistic art theory, an image is neither just the mere depiction of an object, nor a depiction of reality as it can be seen by the human eye, but rather the representation of what is, or was, considered as the ideal form of a certain group of objects. This view did not only lead to the initial rejection of photography as an art form, but likewise presupposed a higher, ideal form which constituted the point of reference for judging the value of any representation of this particular form through the concrete work of art in question. Thus, the abstract, ideal form (the "image") underlies each of its concrete individual representations (the "pictures"). The relationship

180 Pozzo, *Perspectiva pictorum et architectorum*, 1693–1700.

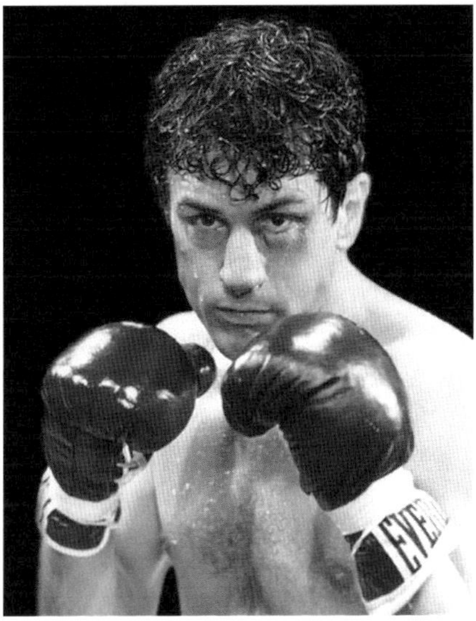

FIGURE 31
Actor Robert de Niro as the boxer Jake LaMotta in the movie "Raging bull" (1980)

also works in the opposite direction in that the concrete representation points to the ideal form after which it was modelled, thus not only representing but also reinforcing the norm it represents. In non-idealistic times, the ideal form is generally informed by the pre-image in the memory of the image designer, which by occupying the place of an idealistic norm, is itself elevated to an image which shows the characteristics of an ideal norm. In other words, it is possible to inflect from the individual picture as a singular "case" to the image as the general "norm" defining what is, and what – or how it – ought to be. Thus, via pictures images repeatedly elevate the visual appearance from the singularity of perception to the universality of the norm. Depending on the object depicted this idealistic display and reinforcement of normative settings can even come in several layers, such as, e.g., in the case of a screenshot of the actor Robert de Niro playing a boxer in the Movie "Raging bull" (Fig. 31).[181] In this case, already the activity of boxing follows its own set of normative rules (e.g., how to correctly hold one's fists), with de Niro following the normative rules of acting that tell him how to properly imitate a real life boxer, while at the same time serving as a role model for the viewers who admire the boxer and/or the actor, or who might aspire to become boxers themselves and repeat the boxing movements as seen in and told by the pictures of the movie.

181 I owe this example to Enrico Terrone from the University of Torino and a co-fellow of mine at the Käte Hamburger Center for Advanced Studies "Law as Culture".

Secondly, the repeated appearance of similar, if not identical pictures in today's mass culture tends to mislead viewers to regard what they have seen not only as "normal" but derive from what appears to be "normal" a "norm" which corresponds to what has normally been seen. In this respect, it can therefore be said that – similarly to legal norms which can be understood as principles of the repeated happening of certain events – the normative effect of images resides in their repeatability and, above all, in their factual repetition, which ensure that images are inscribed into the viewers' memories. Of course, in philosophical terms it is a category error to conclude from a mere frequency of what is seen to its moral correctness, since the one (i.e., what is seen) is of a quantitative nature, whereas the other (i.e., what constitutes the norm), belonging to the realm of ethics, is of a qualitative nature. Of course, the etymological relatedness of "normal" and "norm" indicates that despite their categorical differences both concepts are somehow related, because for practical purposes, what most people do is often – although not always – what is ethically required or at least accepted as moral behaviour. However, it is precisely this categorical error and the normative influence induced by it on the viewer's own role behaviour which is systematically exploited by producers of consumer items when they bombard the prospective buyers with fashion advertisements or other depictions of role models. In this way, these images exercise a normative power on the construction of the body and the self, based on past and existing bodies and selves as well as they design bodies and selves for the future.

It is irrelevant in this respect that images may not be self-executing and that their normative effect is not guaranteed by the threat of coercion by state authorities. What counts in this respect is that the presentation of the norm encoded in the image invites the viewers to align their behaviour accordingly, to re-model their bodies and reconstruct their selves according to what they have been presented if not as the norm, then at least as normal. In this respect, pictures and the images they represent are not innocent in this respect. Even if one does not go as far as ascribing to them an individual autonomous "agens",[182] the normative effect emanating from images can still be derived from their power to attract the attention and hence the views of the persons passing by, provoking them to react, be it in the form of agreement or of disagreement. Of course, it should not be forgotten that images, which are anyway blurred regarding their meaning, can be read in quite different ways depending on the predisposition of the respective viewer. This is particularly true because of the differentiation of what used to be one public with its fixed set of normative

182 See above 3.2.

rules by an increasing plethora of sub-publics which all have formulated, and are following, their own normative set of rules.[183] The image of an underweight female body can be interpreted as a warning against the dangers of anorexia as well as an invitation to approach one's own body even closer to the not yet achieved and ultimately unattainable ideal of further weight loss, to mention just one of the many examples. But irrespective of their reading, with their inherent normative force images thus form part of societal power relations and the fight for the sovereignty of definition over core concepts of self-definition and social coexistence.

In sum, certain categories of images stand in for certain norms and at the same time each individual picture may be regarded as a specific case representing a certain norm. Although representing a different style of normativity, quite like in law, where statutory rules are fleshed out by cases and judgements, images might likewise be seen as embodying normative rules in the form of different cases or instances. The sequential history of images may thus be construed as a series of normative cases, some affirming and some overruling prior cases. True, the normative quality of images may be more pronounced in some images, and not all images may possess the normative qualities just described in very much the same way. It suffices, however, to state that images do potentially carry in themselves a normative force. As stated above, the question of the normative regulation of images thus reveals the double meaning of "regulation of images", in that it can be read both as a *genitivus objectivus* and as a *genitivus subjectivus*. Images are not only objects of normative regulation by law, but as subjects they likewise possess and exercise a normative effect.

6.2 *The Image Quality of Law*

Finally, this brings us to the second question of this part, i.e. the question to what extent – in a mirror image way – legal norms can be said to possess a visual quality. Here also several perspectives can be taken.

First, one might focus on the use of linguistic metaphors both in statutory language and in the language used by judges in their decisions as well as in legal literature when it comes to explaining and construing the normative contents of legal norms.[184] Second, on a more fundamental level, one might inquire about the relationship between the images which precede any norm-setting activity, because before a norm can be formulated, a perception has to exist regarding what that norm should be. However, since the first of these issues relates to a linguistic analysis which falls into the realm of studies in law

183 See above 4.2.

184 For an overview see, e.g., Münkler (2016).

and literature rather than in law and images, and since the second issue is a fundamental methodological problem of legal philosophy, these two perspectives shall only briefly be mentioned here for the sake of completeness.

Rather, attention should be directed at the third perspective which enquires about the quality of law and legal norms as visual images. Of course, in its written form legal rules cannot in and of themselves be regarded as images, but only as representations of underlying ideas. Yet, it is submitted here for discussion that the written text of at least some legal norms – particularly those of an "if"-"then" structure – can be described as representations of visual images and can hence be themselves represented in a visual form. The key to this understanding is to be found in the concept of a "model", a concept generally used in the arts, and in the natural sciences, in engineering and in economics, but hardly ever in the legal context.[185] Even if the term "model" may have different meanings in individual scientific disciplines,[186] any modelling activity – the life model of an artist as well as the models in science – aims at identifying the structures that are considered fundamental for the context to be investigated with the aim of gaining a better understanding of the functioning of those components of reality which are mapped in the model. In epistemological terms, a model can therefore only be developed based on a prior idea of which components of what is to be examined considered might have a bearing on the hypothesis to be tested by making use of the respective model. It therefore seems indeed possible to understand a model as an image of reality in the wider sense in which the complex reality is stripped of all features which are considered insignificant from the point of view of the respective questions asked and the answers to be obtained.

But does this understanding of a model as an image in the wider sense lead to the conclusion that it might likewise be justified to understand a legal norm

185 Throughout legal literature, the keyword "model" is not to be found as an entry in the indexes of descriptions and textbooks of the philosophy and methodology of law; for German books on the philosophy and the methodology of law see only Engisch (2010); Rüthers/Fischer/Birk (2015); Mahlmann (2015). – A notable exception is Vesting (2018), however only with regard to the opposition of 'the model of application and subsumtion' (interpretation which deductively interprets only what is already laid down in the norm) to the 'model of specification' (the interpretation of legal rules which produces new law) which, together, he calls 'rule-application models' that are concerned with the relationship between the norm and the concrete set of facts to which the norm is applied and with regard to which the rule finds its practical application, rather than between the rule and the desired behavior for which the notion of 'model' is used here; see ibid., pp. 31, 38, 110 et seq. and 126.

186 On the origin, development and different uses made of the notion of "model", see Mahr (2003).

as a representation of a model and, hence, as based on, an image in the wider sense? In my opinion, this question may be answered in the affirmative, since the procedure of defining a normative rule in an abstract way for a multitude of individual, concrete events very much resembles the production of an abstract model of the diverse, colourful and three-dimensional world in the form of a two-dimensional, sequential textual sequence of a legal norm. Quite like in the case of modelling in the natural sciences and in economics, not all but only those special features of the factual situation to be regulated are selected as parts of the legal norm which the norm giver considers as important. All other details, which may likewise play a role in individual cases, are ignored. As formulated by Douzinas, law is indeed "predicated upon a cleansing or purificatory operation".[187]

This activity of purificatory modelling shall briefly be demonstrated by the example of the section of the German Civil Code which defines the conditions for legal liability for tortious acts. As stated in Section 823 (1) of the German Civil Code, "[a] person who, intentionally or negligently, unlawfully injures the life, body, health, freedom, property or another right of another person is liable to make compensation to the other party for the damage arising from this."[188] Here, the individual elements of the legal norm – i.e., "who", "property", etc., "of another person", "unlawfully", "injures" and "damage" – are placeholders (variables) for all individual persons, each individual property, each individual other person, each concrete damage, etc. that appear in real life and which can be subsumed, i.e. assigned to the abstract individual elements of the legal norm. In other words, the individual components of the respective concrete facts can be described as elements of the classes of the abstract placeholders of the legal norm. At the same time, the legal norm describes relationships between the parties and the objects involved – a person infringes an object of protection of another person; the infringer is obliged to compensate the injured party for the damage suffered by the injured party under the circumstances mentioned, etc. –, i.e., it models them. Just as the modelling activities in the natural sciences and economics which use standardized symbolic modelling languages such as the graphical "Unified Modelling Language" (UML) developed in informatics in order to visualize software specifications, constructions and documentations, the legal modelling of the relevant real-life facts and relationships can be visually represented with the help of a structural drawing that combines text and graphic elements (Fig. 32).

---

187 Douzinas, in: Douzinas/Nead (1999), p. 3–4; similarly, Braun (2011), pp. 45 and 381 et seq.

188 Translation from the official governmental website, www.gesetze-im-internet.de/englisch_bgb/englisch_bgb.html#p3489.

German Civil Code, § 823 (1) BGB:
"A person who, intentionally or negligently, unlawfully injures the life, body, health, freedom, property or another right of another person is liable to make compensation to the other party for the damage arising from this."

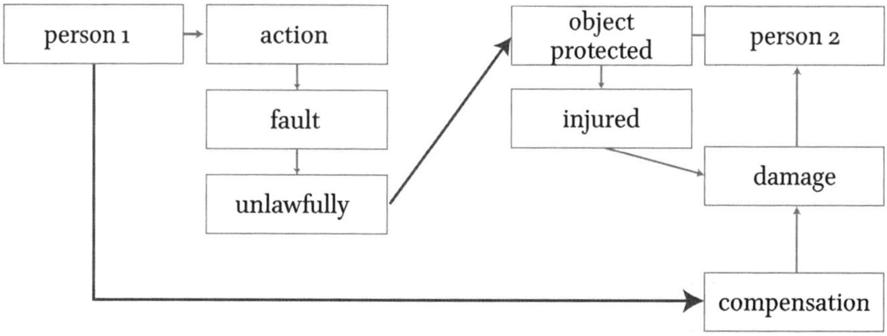

FIGURE 32 Structural drawing of the German tort law provision imposing an obligation onto the infringer to pay damages to the injured party

It might be added that it is well possible to use the words "image" and "model" in relation to legal norms and legal actions in three additional ways. Firstly, as explained above, the norm itself is already a representation of the structural model, which is distilled by the norm giver through the mental activity of structuring the multitude of life facts prior to formulating the norm in text form on paper. Secondly, and more importantly, the legal norm specifies the pattern according to which the norm addressees are told to behave. In other words, their actions are regarded as being in conformity with the norm and do not trigger the legal consequence likewise circumscribed in the norm, whenever the actions replicate and are in conformity with the model of the behaviour as it ought to be shown. Finally, in an even broader sense of "depicting", one might understand not only legal norms, but also court hearings and judgments as images of an event, since they all re-tell, re-count, re-depict – and, at times, even re-enact – prior actions within the framework of judicial processing.[189]

189 Schürmann (2017).

References

Albus, V.: *Bauzaunkunst*, in: Jaeger, F. (ed.), Transparenz und Würde, Berlin 2014, pp. 140–143.

v. Amelunxen, H. (ed.): *Theorie der Fotografie IV*, Munich 2000.

v. Amelunxen, H./Iglhaut, S./Rötzer, F.: *Die Fotografie nach der Fotografie*, Dresden/Basel 1995.

Andina, T.: *Goodbye Beauty – Normativity in Contemporary Visual Arts*, in: Gephart, W./Leko, J. (eds.), Law and the Arts – Elective Affinities and Relationships of Tension, Frankfurt/M. 2017, pp. 47–62.

Anker, E. S./Meyler, B.: *New Directions in Law and Literature*, Oxford 2017.

Assmann, A.: *Erinnerungsräume – Formen und Wandlungen des kulturellen Gedächtnisses*, Munich 1999 (cited after the special edition, Munich 2003).

Banksy: *Wall and piece*, London 2006.

Bauman, Z./Lyon, D.: *Liquid Surveillance – A Conversation*, Cambridge 2012.

Beck, T.S.: *Shaping Images – Scholarly Perspectives on Image Manipulation*, Berlin/Boston 2016.

Beiersdorf, L. (ed.): *Licht und Leinwand – Malerei und Fotografie im 19. Jahrhundert*, Nürnberg 2018.

Belting, H.: *Face and Mask – A Double History*, Princeton/Oxford 2017.

Belting, H. (ed.): *Bilderfragen – Die Bildwissenschaften im Aufbruch*, Munich 2007.

Belting, H.: *Das echte Bild – Bildfragen als Glaubensfragen*, Munich 2005.

Belting, H.: *An Anthropology of Images – Picture, Medium, Body*, Princeton 2011 (German original: *Bild-Anthropologie – Entwürfe für eine Bildwissenschaft*, Munich 2001).

Belting, H.: *Spiegel der Welt – Die Erfindung des Gemäldes in den Niederlanden*, Munich 1994.

Belting, H.: *Likeness and Presence – A History of the Image before the Era of Art*, Chicago 1997.

Benjamin, W.: *The Work of Art in the Age of Mechanical Reproduction* (cited after the German original: *Das Kunstwerk im Zeitalter seiner technischen Reproduzierbarkeit*, version of 1937, in: Tiedemann, R./Schweppenhäuser, H. (ed.): Walter Benjamin, Gesammelte Schriften, 1971–1989, Vol. 1, pp. 471–508).

Beyer, A.: *Die Kunst – zur Sprache gebracht*, Berlin 2017.

Blanke, B./Giannone, A./Vaillant, P.: *Semiotik*, in: Sachs-Hombach (ed.), Bildwissenschaften – Disziplinen, Themen, Methoden, Frankfurt/M. 2005, pp. 149–162.

Blufarb, R.: *Geschichten im Recht – Zur Übertragbarkeit von "Law as Narrative" auf die deutsche Rechtsordnung*, Baden-Baden 2017.

Boehm, G.: *Iconic Turn – Ein Brief*, in: Belting, H. (ed.), Bilderfragen – Die Bildwissenschaften im Aufbruch, Munich 2007, pp. 27–36 (2007a).

Boehm, G.: *Wie Bilder Sinn erzeugen – Die Macht des Zeigens*, Berlin 2007.

Boehm, G. (ed.): Was ist ein Bild?, 4th edition, Munich 2006.

Boehme-Neßler, V. (ed.): *Die Öffentlichkeit als Richter – Litigation-PR als neue Methode der Rechtsfindung*, Baden-Baden 2010.

Boström, J./Jäger, G. (eds.): *Kann Fotografie unsere Zeit in Bilder fassen? – Eine zeitkritische Bilanz*, Bielefeld 2004.

Blasche, S./Gutmann, M./Weingarten, M.: *Repræsentatio Mundi – Bilder als Ausdruck und Aufschluss menschlicher Weltverhältnisse. Historisch-systematische Perspektiven*, Bielefeld 2004.

Bredekamp, H.: *Der Behemoth – Metamorphosen des Anti-Leviathan*, Berlin 2016.

Bredekamp, H.: *Politische Ikonologie des Grundgesetzes*, in: Stolleis, M. (ed.): Herzkammern der Republik – Die Deutschen und das Bundesverfassungsgericht, Munich 2011, pp. 9–35.

Bredekamp, H.: *Image Acts – A Systematic Approach to Visual Agency*, Berlin 2018 (cited after the German original edition: *Theorie des Bildaktes*, Berlin 2010).

Brodocz, A.: *Bilderfeindliche Verfassungsgerichte – Zur Gedächtnispolitik des Bundesverfassungsgerichts und des Supreme Court*, in: Joly, J./Vismann, C./Weitin, T. (eds.): Bildregime des Rechts, Stuttgart 2007, pp. 180–208.

Bruhn, M.: *Bildkritik als Rechtsproblem*, in: Joly, J./Vismann, C./Weitin, T. (eds.): Bildregime des Rechts, Stuttgart 2007, pp. 289–310.

Burnett, R.: *How Images Think*, Cambridge/Mass. 2004.

Castendyk, O.: *Fotorecht*, 2. Aufl., Berlin 2012.

Chéroux, C.: *Paparazzi! – Photographers, Stars, Artists*, Paris 2014.

Christe, Y.: *Das Jüngste Gericht*, Regensburg 2001.

Christian, A.: *Piktogramme – Tendenzen in der Gestaltung und im Einsatz grafischer Symbole*, Cologne 2017.

Clark, C.: *The answer to the machine is in the machine*, in: Hugenholtz, P.B. (ed.), The future of copyright in a digital environment, Alphen aan den Rijn 1996, pp. 139–145.

Cooper, C.: *Hyperides and the Trial of Phryne*, Phoenix, Vol. 49, No. 4, Toronto 1995, pp. 303–318.

Currie, G.: *Image and Mind – Film, Philosophy and Cognitive Science*, Cambridge 1995.

Dahlberg, L. (ed.): *Visualizing law and authority – Essays on legal aesthetics*, Berlin/Boston 2012.

Derrida, J./Stiegler, B.: *Echographies of Television – Filmed Interviews*, Cambridge 2002.

Desai, D.R./Kroll, J.: *Trust but verify – A Guide to Algorithms and the Law*, Harvard Journal of Law and Technology, Vol. 31, No. 1, Fall 2017, pp. 1–64.

Deutscher, G.: *Through the Language Glass – Why the World Looks Different in Other Languages*, London 2010.

Douzinas, C./Nead, L. (eds.): *Law and the Image – The Authority of Art and the Aesthetics of Law*, Chicago 1999.

Dreier, T.: *Bild und Recht – Versuch einer programmatischen Grundlegung*, Baden-Baden 2019.

Dreier, T.: *Citation and Partial Copying*, in: Annual Review of Law and Ethics, Vol. 26 (2018), pp. 39–55.

Dreier, T.: *Law and Images – Normative Models of Representation and Abstraction*, in: Gephart, W./Leko, J. (eds.), Law and the Arts – Elective Affinities and Relationships of Tension, Frankfurt 2017, pp. 155–176.

Dreier, T.: *Technische Entwicklung, Innovation und Recht – Zur Rolle des Patentrechts in der Frühzeit der Fotografie*, in Götting, H.-P./Schlüter, C. (eds.), Nourriture de l'Esprit – Festschrift für Dieter Stauder zum 70. Geburtstag, Baden-Baden 2011, pp. 40–52.

Dreier, T./Becker, J. (eds.): *Urheberrecht und digitale Technologie*, Baden-Baden 1994.

Elkins, J.: *The Object Stares Back – On the Nature of Seeing*, San Diego/New York/London 1996.

Engisch, K.: *Einführung in das juristische Denken*, 11th edition, Stuttgart 2010.

Flusser, V.: *Towards A Philosophy of Photography*, Göttingen 1984.

Foucault, M.: *Discipline and Punish – The Birth of the Prison*, New York 1975.

Franke, H.W.: *Leonardo 2000 – Kunst im Zeitalter des Computers*, Frankfurt/M. 1987.

Frankenberg, G./Niesen, P. (eds.), *Bilderverbot – Recht, Ethik und Ästhetik der öffentlichen Darstellung*, Münster 2004.

Freedberg, D.: *The Power of Images*, Chicago 1989.

Fuhrmann, M.: *Bildung – Europas kulturelle Identität*, Stuttgart 2002.

Ganz, D./Thürlemann, F. (eds.): *Das Bild im Plural*, Berlin 2010.

Gayken, S./Kurz, C. (eds.): *1984.exe – Gesellschaftliche, politische und juristische Aspekte moderner Überwachungstechnologien*, Bielefeld 2008.

Geimer, P.: *Theorien der Fotografie*, Hamburg 2009.

van Gelder, H./Westgeest, H.: *Photography Theory in Historical Perspective*, Chichester 2011.

Gephart, W./Leko, J.: *Introduction*, in: Gephart, W./Leko, J. (eds.), Law and the Arts – Elective Affinities and Relationships of Tension, Frankfurt/M. 2017, pp. 7–22 (2017a).

Gephart, W./Leko, J. (eds.): *Law and the Arts – Elective Affinities and Relationships of Tension*, Frankfurt/M. 2017.

Gerling, W./Holschbach, S./Löffler, P.: *Bilder teilen – Fotografische Praktiken in der digitalen Kultur*, Bielefeld 2017.

Gerz, J.: *Platz der Grundrechte Karlsruhe*, Nürnberg 2006.

Girardin, D./Pirker, Ch. (eds.): *Controversies – A Legal and Ethical History of Photography*, Paris 2012.

Golan, T.: *Sichtbarkeit und Macht – Maschinen als Augenzeugen*, in: Geimer, P. (ed.): Ordnungen der Sichtbarkeit – Fotografie in Wissenschaft, Kunst und Technologie, Frankfurt/M. 2002, pp. 171–210.

Gombrich, E.H.: *The Image & The Eye – Further Studies in the Psychology of Pictorial Representation*, London/New York 1982.

Gombrich, E.H.: *Art and Illusion – A Study in the Psychology of Pictorial Representation*, London 1959.

González García, J.M.: *The Eyes of Justice – Blindfolds and Farsightedness, Vision and Blindness in the Aesthetics of the Law*, Frankfurt/M. 2017.

Goodman, N.: *Languages of Art*, Indianapolis 1968, and 2nd ed. 1976.

Goodrich, P.: *Imago Decidendi – On the Common Law of Images*, Leiden/Boston 2017.

Goodrich, P.: *Legal Emblems and the Art of Law – Obiter depicta as the Vision of Governance*, Cambridge 2013.

Grimm, P./Rhein, S./Müller, M.: *Porno im Web 2.0 – Die Bedeutung sexualisierter Webinhalte in der Lebenswelt von Jugendlichen*, Berlin 2010.

Gross, L./Katz, J.S./Ruby, J. (eds.), *Image Ethics in the Digital Age*, Minnesota/London 2003.

Haarmann, H.: *Universalgeschichte der Schrift*, Frankfurt/M. 1990.

Harth, M./Steinbrenner, J. (eds.): *Bilder als Gründe*, Cologne 2013.

Haus der Geschichte der Bundesrepublik Deutschland (ed.), *Bilder die lügen*, Bonn 1998.

Heil, A./Brehm, M./Ohrt, R.: *Aby Warburg, Mnemosyne Bilderatlas – Rekonstruktion, Kommentar, Aktualisierung*, Karlsruhe 2016.

Heller, C.: *Post-Privacy*, Munich 2011.

Hempel, L./Metelmann, J. (eds.): *Bild, Raum, Kontrolle – Videoüberwachung als Zeichen gesellschaftlichen Wandels*, Frankfurt/M. 2005.

Herbort, N.E.: *Digitale Bildnisse*, Tübingen 2017.

Herder, B.: *Bild und Fiktion – Eine Untersuchung über die Funktion von Bildern in der Erkenntnistheorie*, Cologne 2017.

Hiebaum, C./Knaller, S./Pichler, D. (eds.): *Law and Literature In-Between – Contemporary Inter- and Transdisciplinary Approaches*, Bielefeld 2015.

Hilgendorf, E. (ed.): *Beiträge zur Rechtsvisualisierung*, Berlin 2005.

Hoeren, T./Nielen, M. (eds.): *Fotorecht – Recht der Aufnahme, Gestaltung und Verwertung von Bildern*, Berlin 2004.

Hoerster, N.: *Was ist Recht? – Grundfragen der Rechtsphilosophie*, Munich 2006.

Hoffman, D.D.: *Visual Intelligence – How we create what we see*, New York 1998.

Hopkins, R.: *Picture, Image and Experience: A Philosophical Inquiry*, Cambridge 1998.

Houkes, W.: *Licensed to Share? – How not to (Re-)Balance Rights for Digital Goods*, in: Annual Review of Law and Ethics, Vol. 26 (2018), pp. 209–223.

Hyman, J./Bantinaki, K.: *"Depiction"*, in: Zalta, E.N. (ed.), The Stanford Encyclopedia of Philosophy (Summer 2017 Edition), https://plato.stanford.edu/archives/sum2017/entries/depiction.

Jaeger, F. (ed.), *Transparenz und Würde*, Berlin 2014.

Jay, M.: *Must Justice Be Blind? – The Challenge of Images to the Law*, in: Douzinas, C./Nead, L. (eds.): Law and the Image – The Authority of Art and the Aesthetics of Law, Chicago 1999, pp. 19–35.

Joly, J.-B.: Vorwort, in: Joly, J.-B./Vismann, C./Weitin, T. (eds.): *Bildregime des Rechts*, Stuttgart 2007, pp. 10–14.

Joly, J.-B./Vismann, C./Weitin, T. (eds.): *Bildregime des Rechts*, Stuttgart 2007.

Kammerer, D.: *Bilder der Überwachung*, Frankfurt/M. 2008.

Kandel, E.: *The age of insight – The quest to understand the unconscious in art, mind, and brain, from Vienna 1900 to the present*, New York 2012.

Karallus, C.: *Bildattacken – Die Fotografie vor Gericht um 1900*, in: Joly, J./Vismann, C./Weitin, T. (eds.): Bildregime des Rechts, Stuttgart 2007, pp. 149–170.

Keller, K.: *Der Star und seine Nutzer – Starkult und Identität in der Massengesellschaft*, Bielefeld 2008.

Kemp, W. (ed.): *Theorie der Fotografie I-III*, Munich 1980–1983.

Kern, J.: *"diligite iustitiam" – „Liebet die Gerechtigkeit!" – Rechtsvisualisierung aus kunsthistorischer Sicht*, in: Hilgendorf, E. (ed.): Beiträge zur Rechtsvisualisierung, Berlin 2005, pp. 1–17.

Keyif, S./Korintenberg, B./Zhang, G. (eds.): *Datumsoria – The Return of the Real*, exhibition brochure, Karlsruhe 2017.

Koch, A.: *Handbuch zum Fotorecht*, Sinzheim/Baden 2003.

Kocher, G.: *Zeichen und Symbole des Rechts – Eine historische Ikonografie*, Munich 1992.

Köhler, A.: *Scham und Schamlosigkeit*, Zürich 2013.

Kohl, K.-H.: *Die Macht der Dinge – Geschichte und Theorie sakraler Objekte*, Munich 2003.

Korinek, K.: *Staat und Kunst*, Paderborn 2006.

Kreuzbauer, G.: *Visualisierung juristischer Argumentation*, in: Hilgendorf, E. (ed.): Beiträge zur Rechtsvisualisierung, Berlin 2005, pp. 189–215.

Kurz, C.: *Biometrie nicht nur an den Grenzen – Erkennungsdienstliche Behandlung für Jedermann*, in: Gayken, S./Kurz, C. (eds.): 1984.exe – Gesellschaftliche, politische und juristische Aspekte moderner Überwachungstechnologien, Bielefeld 2008, pp. 101–113.

Lachenmaier, *Die Law as Literature-Bewegung – Entstehung, Entwicklung und Nutzen*, Berlin 2008.

Ladeur, K.-H.: *Das Medienrecht und die Ökonomie der Aufmerksamkeit*, Cologne 2007.

Leitner, W.: *Bilder zu Beweiszwecken im Strafprozess*, in: Joly, J./Vismann, C./Weitin, T. (eds.): Bildregime des Rechts, Stuttgart 2007, pp. 171–179.

Lessig, L.: *Code and other Laws of Cyberspace*, New York 1999.

Liebert, W.-A./Metten, T. (eds.): *Mit Bildern lügen*, Cologne 2007.

Liebsch, D./Mößner, N. (eds.): *Visualisierung und Erkenntnis – Bildverstehen und Bildverwenden in Natur- und Geisteswissenschaften*, Cologne 2012.

Luhmann, N.: *Theory of Society*, Stanford 2003 (German original: *Die Gesellschaft der Gesellschaft*, Frankfurt/M. 1997).

Luhmann, N.: *Law as a Social System*, Oxford 2004 (German original: *Das Recht der Gesellschaft*, Frankfurt/M. 1993).

Lunenfeld, P.: *Digitale Fotografie – Das dubitative Bild*, in: Stiegler, B. (ed.): Texte zur Theorie der Fotografie, Stuttgart 2010, pp. 344–361.

Maar, C./Burda, H. (eds.): *Iconic Turn – Die neue Macht der Bilder*, Cologne 2004.

Mahlmann, M.: *Rechtsphilosophie und Rechtstheorie*, 3rd edition, Baden-Baden 2015.

Mahr, B.: *Modellieren – Beobachtungen und Gedanken zur Geschichte des Modellbegriffs*, in: Krämer, S./Bredekamp, H. (eds.): Bild – Schrift – Zahl, Munich 2003, pp. 59–86.

Manderson, D. (ed.): *Law and the Visual – Representations, Technologies, and Critique*, Toronto/Buffalo/London 2018.

Marek, K.: *Ikonoklastische Vereinnahmung – Rechtstheoretische Regime des Bildes*, in: Joly, J./Vismann, C./Weitin, T. (eds.): Bildregime des Rechts, Stuttgart 2007, pp. 45–61.

Mayer-Schönberger, V.: *Delete – The Virtue of Forgetting in the Digital Age*, Princeton 2009.

McClure, L.: *Courtesans at Table – Gender and Greek Literary Culture in Athenaeus*, New York 2003.

Mensa, D.L.: *Radar Imaging*, International Journal of Imaging Systems and Technology 4, no. 3 (1992), pp. 148–163 (cited after Elkin (1996), p. 69).

Michalos, C.: *The Law of Photography and Digital Images*, London 2004.

Mitchell, W.J.T.: *Pictorial Turn – Eine Antwort*, in: Belting, H. (ed.), Bilderfragen – Die Bildwissenschaften im Aufbruch, Munich 2007, pp. 37–46.

Mitchell, W.J.T.: *What do pictures want? – The Lives and Loves of Images*, Chicago 2005.

Mitchell, W.J.T.: *The Reconfigured Eye – Visual Truth in the Post-photographic Era*, Cambridge/Mass. 1992 (1992a).

Mitchell, W.J.T.: *The Pictorial Turn*, Art Forum, March 1992, pp. 89–94.

Mittelberger, F./Pelz, S./Rosen, M./Franke, A. (eds.): *Maschinensehen – Feldforschung in den Räumen bildgebender Technologien*, Karlsruhe 2013.

Mori, M./MacDorman, K.F./Kageki, N., *The Uncanny Valley*, IEEE Robotics & Automation Magazine, Vol. 19 (2012), pp. 98–100.

Müller, M.: *Grundlagen der visuellen Kommunikation*, Konstanz 2003.

Müller, W.: *Kunstwerk, Kunstgeschichte und Computer*, Munich 1987.

Münkler, L.: *Metaphern im Recht – Zur Bedeutung organischer Vorstellungen von Staat und Recht*, Der Staat 2016, pp. 181–211.

Nagel, T.: *Concealment and Exposure & Other Essays*, Oxford 2002.

Nake, F.: *Algorithmus, Bild und Pixel – Das Bild im Blickfeld der Informatik*, in: Sachs-Hombach, K. (ed.): Bildwissenschaft – Zwischen Reflexion und Anwendung, Cologne 2005, pp. 101–121.

Netzwerk Bildphilosophie (ed.): *Bild und Methode – Theoretische Hintergründe und methodische Verfahren der Bildwissenschaft*, Cologne 2014.

Ortland, E./Dreier, T./Schmücker, R. (eds.): *Handwörterbuch Original und Kopie*, Stuttgart (forthcoming).

Pichler, W./Ubl, R.: *Bildtheorie – zur Einführung*, Hamburg 2014.

Pohlmann, U./v. Hohenzollern, J.G. (eds.): *Eine neue Kunst? Eine andere Natur! – Fotografie und Malerei im 19. Jahrhundert*, Munich 2004.

Posner, R.A.: *Law and Literature*, 3rd edition, Cambridge/Mass. 2009.

Prange, R.: *Lemma "Bild"*, in: Pfisterer, U. (ed.), Metzler Lexikon Kunstwissenschaft – Ideen, Methoden, Begriffe, Stuttgart/Weimar 2003, pp. 43–46.

Presse Informations AG (PIAG) (ed.): *Bestseller Photos*, Sinzheim 2004.

Quanter, R.: *Die Sittlichkeitsverbrechen im Laufe der Jahrhunderte und ihre strafrechtliche Beurteilung*, Amsterdam 1925 (reprint, Wiesbaden 2003).

Raabe, O./Oberle, D./Baumann, C./Wacker, R./Funk, C.: *Recht ex machina – Formalisierung des Rechts im Internet der Dienste*, Berlin/Heidelberg 2012.

Resnik, J./Curtis, D.: *Representing Justice – Invention, Controversy, and Rights in City-States and Democratic Courtrooms*, New Haven 2011.

Rifkin, J., *The Age of Access*, New York 2000.

Rimmele, M./Sachs-Hombach, K./Stiegler, B. (eds.).: *Bildwissenschaft und Visual Culture*, Bielefeld 2014.

Rimmele, M./Stiegler, B.: *Visuelle Kulturen – Visual Culture*, Hamburg 2012.

Robbins, P., *Modularity of Mind*, in: Zalte, E.N. (ed.), The Stanford Encyclopedia of Philosophy, Winter 2017, https://plato.stanford.edu/archives/win2017/entries/modularity-mind.

Röhl, K.F.: *Rechtswissenschaft*, in: Sachs-Hombach, K. (ed.): Bildwissenschaft – Disziplinen, Themen, Methoden, Frankfurt/M. 2005, pp. 247–256.

Röhl, K.F./Ulbrich, S.: *Recht anschaulich – Visualisierung der Juristenausbildung*, Cologne 2007.

Rössler, B.: *Der Wert des Privaten*, Frankfurt/M. 2001.

Rouge-Ducos, I.: *Imperator*, in: Fleckner, U./Warnke, M./Ziegler, H. (eds.), Handbuch der politischen Ikonographie, Munich 2011, Vol. 2, pp. 7–13.

Rouillé, A.: *La photographie – entre document et art contemporain*, Paris 2005.

Rüthers, B./Fischer, C./Birk, A.: *Rechtstheorie*, 8th edition, Munich 2015.

Sachs-Hombach, K. (ed.): *Das Bild als kommunikatives Medium – Elemente einer allgemeinen Bildwissenschaft*, 3rd edition, Cologne 2013.

Sachs-Hombach, K.: *Vom Text zum Bild – Wege für das Recht*, in: Hilgendorf, E. (ed.): Beiträge zur Rechtsvisualisierung, Berlin 2005, pp. 163–176 (2005c).

Sachs-Hombach, K. (ed.): *Bildwissenschaft – Zwischen Reflexion und Anwendung*, Cologne 2005 (2005b).

Sachs-Hombach, K.: *Konzeptionelle Rahmenüberlegungen zur interdisziplinären Bildwissenschaft*, in: Sachs-Hombach, K. (ed.): Bildwissenschaft – Disziplinen, Themen, Methoden, Frankfurt/M. 2005, pp. 11–20 (2005a).

Sachs-Hombach, K. (ed.): *Bildwissenschaft – Disziplinen, Themen, Methoden*, Frankfurt/M. 2005.

Sachs-Hombach, K.: *Das Bild als kommunikatives Medium – Elemente einer allgemeinen Bildwissenschaft*, Cologne 1993.

Sachs-Hombach, K./Schirra, J.R.J. (eds.): *Origins of Pictures – Anthropological Discourses in Image Science*, Cologne 2013.

Sachs-Hombach, K./Totzke, R. (eds.): *Bilder, Sehen, Denken – Zum Verhältnis von begrifflich-philosophischen und empirisch-psychologischen Ansätzen in der bildwissenschaftlichen Forschung*, Cologne 2011.

Samuelson, P.: *DRM {and, or, vs.} the Law*, Communications of the ACM 46, No. 4, 2003, pp. 41–45.

Schaar, P.: *Das Ende der Privatsphäre – Der Weg in die Überwachungsgesellschaft*, Munich 2007.

Schild, W.: *Bilder von Recht und Gerechtigkeit*, Cologne 1995.

Schirra, J.R.J.: *Computervisualistik*, in: Sachs-Hombach (eds.), Bildwissenschaften – Disziplinen, Themen, Methoden, Frankfurt/M. 2005, pp. 268–280.

Schneider, U.F.: *Der Januskopf der Prominenz – zum ambivalenten Verhältnis von Privatheit und Öffentlichkeit*, Wiesbaden 2004.

Schricker, G./Loewenheim, U. (eds.): *Urheberrecht*, 5th edition, Munich 2017.

Schübel, E.: *Wie sollten wir – auch mit Blick auf die Rechte der Verfahrensbeteiligten – mit dem EMöGG umgehen?*, in: Der Bundesgerichtshof im Spiegel der Öffentlichkeit, 6. Karlsruher Strafrechtsdialog, Karlsruhe 2017, pp. 35–38.

Schürmann, E.: Law as the Art of Picturing a Case, in: Gephart, W./Leko, J. (eds.), Law and the Arts – Elective Affinities and Relationships of Tension, Frankfurt/M. 2017, pp. 25–38.

Schulz, M.: *Ordnungen der Bilder*, Munich 2005.

Schuster, M.: *Bilder des Rechts, die Justitia und die Rechtsgewalt*, in: Hilgendorf, E. (ed.): Beiträge zur Rechtsvisualisierung, Berlin 2005, pp. 177–187.

Sennett, R.: *The Fall of Public Man*, New York 1974.

Seja, S.: *Handlungstheorien des Bildes*, Cologne 2009.

Siebenpfeiffer, H.: *"Kriminelle Körper" – Zeichen und Verbrechen bei Lavater, Lombroso und Kafka*, in: Joly, J./Vismann, C./Weitin, T. (eds.): Bildregime des Rechts, Stuttgart 2007, pp. 109–148.

Sloterdijk, P.: *Neue Zeilen und Tage – Notizen 2011–2013*, Berlin 2018.

Sloterdijk, P.: *Sphären III – Schäume, Plurale Sphärologie*, Frankfurt/M. 2004.

Sörensen, E. (ed.), Cultures of Computer Game Concerns – The Child Across Families, Law, Science and Industry, Bielefeld 2018.

Sofsky, W.: *Verteidigung des Privaten*, Munich 2007.

Sontag, S.: *On photography*, New York 1977.

Specht, L.: *Diktat der Technik – Rematerialisierung der Privatautonomie im informationstechnologischen Umfeld*, Baden-Baden 2019.

Steinhauer, F.: *Das eigene Bild – Verfassungen der Bildrechtsdiskurse um 1900*, Berlin 2013.

Steinhauer, F.: *Bildregeln – Studien zum juristischen Bilderstreit*, Munich 2009.

Steinhauer, F.: *Das Recht am eigenen Bild in den Kollisionen der Sichtbarkeit*, in: Joly, J./Vismann, C./Weitin, T. (eds.): Bildregime des Rechts, Stuttgart 2007, pp. 222–246.

Steller, *Computer und Kunst – Programmierte Gestaltung, Wurzeln und Tendenzen neuer Ästhetiken*, Mannheim et al. 1992.

Stiegler, B. (ed.): *Texte zur Theorie der Fotografie*, Stuttgart 2010.

Stiegler, B.: *Montagen des Realen – Photographie als Reflexionsmedium und Kulturtechnik*, Munich 2009.

Stiegler, B.: *Theoriegeschichte der Photographie*, Munich 2006 (2006a).

Stiegler, B.: *Bilder der Fotografie – Ein Album photographischer Metaphern*, Frankfurt/M. 2006.

Stolleis, M.: *The Eye of the Law – Two Essays on Legal History*, London 2009 (cited after the German original edition: *Das Auge des Gesetzes – Geschichte einer Metapher*, Munich 2004).

Strauss, D.L.: *Between the Eyes – Essays on Photography and Politics*, New York, 2003.

Tagg, J.: *The Burden of Representation – Essays on Photographies and Histories*, Minneapolis 1988.

Thiele, J. (ed.): *Die Bilder der Deutschen*, Munich 2005.

Thürlemann, F.: *Mehr als ein Bild – Für eine Kunstgeschichte des hyperimage*, Paderborn 2013.

Ullrich, W.: *Rebloggen als Kulturtechnik*, in: Landwehr, D. (ed.), Public Domain, Basel 2015, pp. 92–103.

Ullrich, W.: *Tiefer hängen – Über den Umgang mit der Kunst*, Berlin 2003.

Vesting, Thomas: *Legal Theory*, Munich 2018.

Virilio, P.: *The Vision Machine*, Bloomington, 1994.

Vismann, C.: *Bildregime des Rechts – Rechtsregime des Bildes*, in: Joly, J./Vismann, C./Weitin, T. (eds.): Bildregime des Rechts, Stuttgart 2007, pp. 15–32.

Vögtli, A./Ernst, B.: *Wissenschaftliche Bilder – Eine kritische Betrachtung*, Basel 2007.

Vogeley, K.: *Neurowissenschaft*, in: Sachs-Hombach (ed.), Bildwissenschaften – Disziplinen, Themen, Methoden, Frankfurt/M. 2005, pp. 97–108.

Walton, K.L.: *Mimesis as Make-Believe*, Cambridge, MA/London 1990.

Walton, K.L.: *Transparent Pictures – On the Nature of Photographic Realism*, Critical Inquiry, Vol. 11, No. 2 (December 1984), pp. 246–277.

Wanckel, E.: *Foto- und Bildrecht*, 5th edition, Munich 2017.

Warnke, M. (ed.): *Aby Warburg – Der Bilderatlas Mnemosyne,* Gesammelte Schriften, Vol. II/1, 2nd edition, Berlin 2003.

Weibel, *Gamma und Amplitude,* Berlin 2004.

Weigel, S.: *Grammatologie der Bilder,* Berlin 2015.

Wiedemann, D.: *Bilder im Zeitalter der digitalen Bildbearbeitung – Neue Ästhetiken und verschwundene Wahrheiten?,* in: Sachs-Hombach, K. (ed.): Bildwissenschaft – Zwischen Reflexion und Anwendung, Cologne 2005, pp. 443–456.

Wielsch, D.: *Zugangsregeln,* Tübingen 2008.

Wiesing, L.: *Die Sichtbarkeit des Bildes – Geschichte und Perspektiven der formalen Ästhetik,* Frankfurt/New York 2008.

Wiesing, L.: *Methoden der Bildwissenschaft,* in: Sachs-Hombach, K. (ed.): Bildwissenschaft – Zwischen Reflexion und Anwendung, Cologne 2005, pp. 144–154 (2005a).

Wiesing, L.: *Artifizielle Präsenz – Studien zur Philosophie des Bildes,* Frankfurt/M. 2005.

Wiesing, L. (ed.): *Philosophie der Wahrnehmung – Modelle und Reflexionen,* Frankfurt/M. 2002.

Wohlfeil, R.: *Geld,* in: Fleckner, U./Warnke, M./Ziegler, H. (eds.), Handbuch der politischen Ikonographie, Munich 2011, Vol. 1, pp. 395–400.

Wolf, H. (ed.): *Paradigma Fotografie – Fotokritik am Ende des fotografischen Zeitalters,* Vol. 2, Frankfurt/M. 2003.

Wolf, H. (ed.): *Paradigma Fotografie – Fotokritik am Ende des fotografischen Zeitalters,* Vol. 1, Frankfurt/M. 2002.

Wolf, N.: *The Beauty Myth,* London 1990.

Wollheim, R.: *Seeing-As, Seeing-In and Pictorial Representation,* in: Wollheim, Art and its Objects, Cambridge 1980, pp. 205–226.

Wortmann, V.: *Authentisches Bild und authentisierende Form,* Cologne 2003.

Würkner, J.: *Das Bundesverfassungsgericht und die Kunst,* Munich 1994.

Wyss, B.: *Vom Bild zum Kunstsystem,* Cologne 2006.

Zimmermann, A.: *Skandalöse Körper – Abject Art vom Surrealismus bis zu den Culture Wars,* Berlin 2001.